The Old Law and the New Law

The Old Law and the New Law

The Old Law &
The New Law
William Barclay

THE SAINT ANDREW PRESS
EDINBURGH

© WILLIAM BARCLAY 1972

Published in 1972
by the Saint Andrew Press
121 George Street, Edinburgh EH2 4YN

ISBN 0 7152 0197 2

Printed by T. and A. Constable Ltd., Edinburgh

CONTENTS

Scripture references are to the Revised Standard Version (RSV). Other versions used are the Authorised Version (AV) and the New English Bible (NEB).

FOREWORD

I am very grateful to the Church of Scotland Publications Committee for republishing this little book. It began life as a Boys' Brigade Handbook and I am glad to see it receive the opportunity to be of wider service. I am most grateful to the Rev. James Martin, B.D., of High Carntyne Church, Glasgow, for the revision work he did on it. This has been of invaluable help. I hope the book will be of use to preachers and teachers and general readers.

The University of Glasgow,
    April 1972

WILLIAM BARCLAY

THE OLD LAW

CHAPTER ONE

The Necessity of Law

If any body of people are going to live together they must
make laws and they must agree to stick by them. That's
what it's like in a game, for instance. We all know that the
person who will not keep its laws simply ruins the game. If
we are playing cricket, and a player is out, and refuses to go
out, then the whole game is spoiled. A player in a football
match who refused to obey the referee would be promptly
and rightly sent off the field.

It is exactly the same with a community and with a nation.
It is impossible to have a nation or a community without
laws and without these laws being kept. To take a simple
example, traffic would become chaos unless motorists agreed
to keep to the correct side of the road, and unless they
obeyed the traffic lights. If we never knew when motorists
were going to drive through the lights when they were red,
then there would be all kinds of accidents every day in life.

It is quite clear that people cannot live together at all
unless they make laws and agree to obey them. We could
put this in another way; it is impossible for a nation to exist
as a nation unless it has its laws.

The people of Israel were slaves in Egypt for four hundred
long and weary years. During that long period they built
great buildings for the Egyptians and were never allowed to
govern themselves; they had no freedom whatsoever. Then
there arose their great deliverer, Moses; and Moses, helped

by God, led them out of Egypt into the desert so that they might set out on their long journey to Palestine, the land which God had promised to them. Up to this time they had been slaves and had to do exactly what they were told to do. They had no liberty; they had no freedom; and they had no responsibility. But now they were on their own; they were on their way to become a nation; and the first thing they needed was a set of laws by which they might live and by which they might become not a rabble but a real community.

This is exactly what they got in the Ten Commandments. The Ten Commandments were the rules of life. By obeying them the people of Israel learned to become a nation. These Ten Commandments are the basis of life not only for the people of Israel; they are the basis by which we still live our lives and by which all life is governed.

Let us set them down one by one:

1. You shall have no other Gods before me.
2. You shall not make yourself a graven image.
3. You shall not take the name of the Lord your God in vain.
4. Remember the sabbath day to keep it holy.
5. Honour your father and your mother.
6. You shall not kill.
7. You shall not commit adultery.
8. You shall not steal.
9. You shall not bear false witness.
10. You shall not covet.

These, then, are the Ten Commandments, the Commandments which made Israel into a nation, and the Commandments which are still the basis of all life.

When we look at these Ten Commandments we see that they fall into four different groups. The first four Commandments deal with our duty to God. The fifth deals with our duty to our parents. The sixth, seventh, eighth and ninth deal with our duty to others. The tenth deals with our duty to ourselves. This is to say that the Ten Commandments set out four areas of life in which we have a special duty.

i. The Commandments begin by laying down our duty to God. This means to say that God has to be given the first place in our duty and in our life. I once knew a man who was the head of a very famous business firm; and when he was interviewing any man with a view to employing him, he did not first of all ask him about his technical qualifications, he did not ask him about his university degrees, he did not ask him about how much he knew or did not know. The first question he asked him was, 'Do you believe in God, and do you go to Church?' This employer, and he was a man with a very big business and a very successful business, felt that the most important thing about a man was to know whether or not he believed in God.

And in this, this employer was perfectly right. If a man believes in God he will always feel that God sees him. If a man believes in God he will always ask, 'What does God want me to do?' If he believes in God he will work not to earn a wage and not to please a human master but to please God. No one is going to argue that a man cannot be a good workman and an honest man unless he believes in God; but it is quite certain that if a man is the kind of workman who always tries to do work in such a way that he can take it and show it to God, then he is the kind of workman that people want. If we put God in the centre of life we cannot ever go far wrong.

ii. The second duty which the Ten Commandments lay down is duty to parents. They tell us to honour our father and our mother. The Old Testament is very stern about this; it actually says that a rebellious son can be put to death (Deuteronomy 21:18-21). The ancient Greeks thought so much of a son's duty to his parents that a son who did not support his parents in their old age could be put into prison and very heavily fined.

We ought to honour our parents for two reasons. First, we owe them our very lives. There was a time when we could do nothing for ourselves, when the slightest blow would have killed us and when we would have died if we had just been left to ourselves. Through all that time they cared for us. We ought to show our gratitude to people to whom we owe our lives. Second, if you are journeying along a road which is dangerous, it is only sensible to take the advice of people who have journeyed along that road before. Life is a dangerous road. Older people have journeyed that road before us and they know the pitfalls and dangers, and it is only wise to listen to what they have to say to us. To refuse to take advice from a person who knows the way may be to choose to get lost and run into trouble. It should not be difficult to honour our parents.

iii. The Ten Commandments tell us of our duty to others. They tell us that we must not harm another person's life or personality; and that we must not rob him of his possessions or of his good name. Life could not go on if people killed each other and stole each other's goods and destroyed each other's good name. In regard to other people there is just one rule for life and Jesus laid it down: we must always act towards others as we would have them act towards us. (Matthew 7:12.)

iv. The last Commandment tells us that we must not covet. This means that we have a duty to ourselves and that duty is to control our wishes and our desires. You could put this in another way. This Commandment says that we should never want what we have no right to want and that we should be content to have what we possess. We cannot change ourselves into other people nor can we possess what others possess. A very great General once said that the whole art of war is to do the best one can with the resources that one has, and that also is the art of life. There is an old fable which tells how a mountain was looking with contempt upon a little squirrel. The squirrel looked up at the mountain and said, 'I cannot carry forests on my back, but you cannot crack a nut.' Each one of us has his own gift and his own talent and we should do the best we can with them and not covet those of other people.

We can never live together without laws and without consenting to keep the laws. The Ten Commandments changed the people of Israel from a crowd into a nation. They tell us of our duty to God, our duty to our parents, our duty to others, and our duty to ourselves, and we are going to look now at each of the Ten Commandments in turn.

For Discussion

Is there anything in our way of life, at home or business, that makes it difficult for us to carry out any of the four duties laid down in the Commandments?

CHAPTER TWO

No Other Gods

The first Commandment is, 'You shall have no other Gods before me' (Exodus 20:3). That is to say, God is to be the only God whom we worship and whom we obey. It took a long time, many, many centuries, for people to discover that there was only one God.

They began by believing in a great many gods. They began by believing that every great power in nature was a god. They saw the sun shining, and felt its heat, and saw it chasing the darkness from the sky, and they said, 'Surely the sun must be a god.' They saw the fire burning: they saw that the fire could burn down a whole forest when it got a grip; and they said to themselves, 'This power is more than human, fire must be a god.' They saw the sea in turmoil; they saw the sea take and toss the greatest and the largest ships until they became wrecks; and they said to themselves, 'Surely this power in the sea is far more than human power, the sea must be a god.'

They looked at the earth and they saw the corn growing and the grapes ripening and the olives growing larger, and they said to themselves, 'What is it that makes these things grow? We can't do it; this must be the power of a god'; and they spoke of the god of growth. So there was a time when people believed in many gods; when they thought that every great power and everything that made things happen was really a god.

Not only did they believe in a great many gods, they also believed in a great many demons. Demons were a kind of halfway house, more than human but not quite gods. We would call them spirits. So they said that every tree had its spirit, and every river had its spirit, and every cave had its spirit, and every hill had its spirit.

But there was one way in which they specially saw these spirits at work. They asked themselves, 'What is it that makes a person ill? What is it that gives a person pain? What is it that makes an epileptic writhe and twist on the ground?' And their answer was that somehow a spirit got into the person and caused the pain and the illness.

A famous doctor has pointed out a fact which shows how strong this belief in spirits was. Sometimes in very old cemeteries, cemeteries in which people were buried almost before history began, they find skulls which have been trepanned. To trepan a person's skull is to bore a little hole through the solid bone. That is a difficult and a serious operation at any time but in ancient times when they had neither instruments nor anæsthetics it must have been a very serious and a very painful operation. Further, the hole is too small to be of any practical medical use and the fact that there is bone formation round the side of the hole shows that it was bored during life. The reason why the hole was bored was to allow the evil spirit to escape from inside the man. The fact that people submitted to this kind of thing in order to try to be rid of the demons shows how intensely they believed in them.

After a while there came a second stage when people believed there were a great many gods but that there was only one for their country. Each country had its god and within the borders of its country that god reigned supreme and must be obeyed. But people believed that when they came to the borders of their country and passed into another country they came under the control of a different god. So in the book of Judges (11:24) we find an occasion on which

Jephthah is talking to the Ammonites; and he says to the Ammonites, 'Will you not possess what Chemosh your god gives you to possess?' What Jephthah is saying is, 'Jehovah, our God, gives us what we have; Chemosh, your god, gives you what you have; would you not be content with that?'

At this stage there were as many gods as there were countries and each country believed that within its borders its own god was supreme, but once you left the country you came under the power of another god.

That was certainly a step forward from the idea of hundreds of different gods, but there was another step still to take. The people had to discover that there was not just one God for a country, but one God for the whole world. How did they come to that belief?

We cannot tell for certain just how they came to it; but we can guess. There came a time when great empires arose, the empires of Assyria, of Babylon, of Persia; and above all the empire of Alexander the Great. Alexander the Great was the man who conquered the whole world; he even led his armies as far away as India; he died when he was only thirty-three and, before he died, he wept because he had no more worlds left to conquer. This kind of thing showed people that the whole world could be one kingdom, and if the whole world could be one kingdom this led their thoughts to the fact that there could be only one God. And so the Psalmist can write (139:7):

> *Whither shall I go from thy Spirit?*
> *Or whither shall I flee from thy presence?*

The Psalmist has come to feel that everywhere he goes God is there.

So the Commandment tells us that we must have only one God. That does not mean that we must, so to speak, theoretically believe that there is one God; almost everyone does that. It means that in our lives we must have only one God.

What would you say your God really is? Your God is really that to which you are prepared to give all your time, all your strength, all your obedience. Your God is that which is most important in your life. There are at least three things that we can make the most important in life.

i. You can make money and material things the most important things in life. Put it this way: suppose someone was to come to you and say, 'Here is a parcel of drugs for which people will pay a very large sum of money. You can have them for nothing and you can sell them for as much as you can get.' The question is, would you say to yourself, 'I want this money and I am going to get it.' Or would you say, 'I cannot possibly take money this way; because it is the wrong thing to do.' Suppose you were given the chance to steal something, something you wanted very much indeed, and suppose you had an absolute guarantee that you would never be found out, would you do it? If you would make money that way and if you would steal things like that, then money and things are your God. If, on the other hand, you would say, 'I can't do that; it's wrong,' then you really do have God as your God.

ii. It is quite possible to make having a good time your God. A student can be so determined to have a good time that he neglects all his studies, he does not care how much anxiety and worry he causes other people, he spends money on having a good time that ought to go to far more serious and far more important things, and the only thing in this world that he really cares for is pleasure. If you live like that then pleasure is your God; but if when you are tempted to do these things you say, 'I can't do that; I've got to live honestly and I have got to make the most of life, and I've got to do the best I can with my talents,' then you are really serving God.

iii. You can make a God of yourself. When you are faced with a choice of different things to do, what do you say? Do you say, 'What do I want to do?' Or do you say, 'What is the right thing to do?' Suppose, for instance, you are offered two jobs. The one with the bigger salary is the kind of job which is no use to anyone, a quite selfish and a quite useless job. The other is a job which will do a great many people a great deal of good, but the pay is far less. Which will you take?

If your standard is always 'What do I want?' then you are making yourself your God. If your standard is, 'What is right?' then you are really serving God.

Few nowadays believe in all kinds of gods; but it is still possible to make a God of money, to make a God of pleasure, to make a God of oneself. The one way to prove that we really and truly believe in the one true God is always to say to him, 'What do you want me to do?'

For Discussion

How can we show in action that we believe in God?

CHAPTER THREE

Worshipping Things Instead of God

The second Commandment says, 'You shall not make for yourself a graven image' (Exodus 20:4). This forbids what is called idolatry, and idolatry is worshipping some kind of image which some man has made.

Is it not surprising that anyone could regard as a god some piece of stone or metal, however precious, however wonderfully carved, or however artistically made.

The Old Testament prophets always condemned idolatry, and one of the great weapons that they used against it was just sheer ridicule. Isaiah (44:9-20) shouts with laughter at the man who takes a block of wood, and with part of it heats his house, and with part of it cooks his dinner, and with part of it makes a god. He pours scorn on the gods that have to be carried about on men's shoulders when they have to be moved (Isaiah 46:5-7). Surely if you have a real and true God, you can expect your God to support and to help you; but if you worship an idol, says Isaiah, you have to support and help it. Jeremiah (10:3-5) talks about gods knocked together with a hammer and nails. And often in the Bible there is contempt for the gods who have eyes and cannot see, who have ears and cannot hear, who have mouths and cannot speak (Deuteronomy 4:28; Psalm 135:15-17). When you put it this way, it does seem extraordinary that anyone should be silly enough to worship an idol which is just a block of wood or a lump of metal.

But when we try to understand how this kind of thing started, it is not quite so silly. It all began because men found it difficult to worship a god they could not see. So they said to themselves, 'We will make something which will represent the god and that will make it easier to think of the god.' In the first instance the idol was never meant to *be* the god; it was meant only to *stand for* the god.

We can perhaps understand it, if we think of it this way. Suppose we have a friend whom we have not seen for a very long time, and suppose we sit down to write a letter to that friend, and suppose we find the letter hard to write, because we have been separated for so long. In such a situation it might well help if we took a photograph of the friend and put it where we could see it, and wrote, as it were, looking at the photograph. The photograph would bring our friend nearer to our mind. At first that is what an idol was meant to do.

The trouble was that men began to worship the idol instead of the god it stood for; men began to worship the symbol instead of the reality it was supposed to represent. It is not really difficult to see how idolatry began, and it is not really so silly as it looks. For all that, we may well be saying, 'I am not likely to do a thing like that.' But perhaps we are more likely to do it than we think.

i. Take a very small thing first of all. Quite a lot of people carry some kind of lucky mascot, some kind of charm. Some carry a lucky penny or a lucky sign of the zodiac, or, for instance, if they go on a journey, they take a St. Christopher sign to avoid accidents. That is really idolatry, for it is believing that in some way the carrying of a little bit of metal or plastic can have an effect on their lives.

ii. But there is something much more serious than that. The real essence of idolatry is that a man worships a thing instead of God.

There is no doubt at all that there is a great deal of that today. People assess their success in life by the number of things which they possess. We think a man a success if he has a big motor car, or an elaborate television set or record-player, or if he can go every year for a Continental holiday.

This is obviously wrong. A clue in a certain crossword puzzle read like this: What makes a home? And the answer was: Furniture. It is not difficult to see that you might have the best and the most expensively furnished house in the country, and yet it might be a very poor home. If there is no love and kindness and comradeship, it will be a poor home, no matter what the furniture is like.

Everyone knows the story of the king who was dying of melancholy. Nothing that the doctors could do would take away his dreadful depression. At last one doctor came forward with a prescription. If the king could manage to get the shirt of a perfectly happy man and wear that, he would be cured. So a search was begun all over the kingdom for a perfectly happy man. At last they found one. He was a tramp on the road, and as happy as the day was long. So they offered him any money he wanted for his shirt. But he only laughed at them, because he was so poor that he had not a shirt to his back. That story is a kind of parable which tells that things are not the most important factors in the world.

We do well, especially when we are young, not to get into the habit of measuring success by the number of things we possess, or the amount of money we can get. It has been said of some people that they know the price of everything and the value of nothing. And most of the most valuable things have not got a price; they cannot be bought for money at all.

iii. It is possible to put this another way. Idolatry is worshipping created things rather than the Creator. In the old days men used to worship the sun and the moon and the stars; but we know that the one we ought to worship is the God who created all these things.

The kind of way in which this enters into our lives is this. There are people who worship physical fitness; but we ought really to worship the God who gave us our bodies and our health. There are people who worship cleverness; but we really ought to worship the God who gave us our minds and made us able to think.

When we enjoy the hills or the seaside or the sunshine, we should be thinking of the God who made them all. When we enjoy our good health, and when we do well at our studies, we should be thinking of the God who gave us our bodies and our minds. We should always see, behind and beyond that which is created, the Creator who made all things, for then we will never fall into any kind of idolatry.

Idolatry is worshipping things instead of God. We must avoid the superstition which thinks that any thing can affect our lives. We must never evaluate life by the number of things that we possess. We must always see the Creator behind the creation.

For Discussion

What is idolatry for us? How may it get into our lives?

CHAPTER FOUR

The Sacredness of a Promise

The third Commandment says: You shall not take the name of the Lord your God in vain (Exodus 20:7). We must begin by being sure of what this commandment is saying. It is not forbidding the use of bad language. Some people use the name of God and of Jesus as oaths in the sense of bad language. That is certainly something that we should not do. But what this commandment forbids is the making of a promise in the name of God, and then breaking it. The commandment is saying: You must never swear by God to do something, you must never pledge yourself in the name of God to some course of action, and then not do it.

When people do take a solemn pledge or make a solemn promise, they frequently do so in the name of God. In a court of law, if a man is a witness, he swears by almighty God to tell the truth, the whole truth and nothing but the truth. At the service of confirmation we are asked, 'Do you *in the presence of God*, and of this congregation, renew the solemn promise and vow that was made in your name at your baptism?' When we become members of the Church of Scotland we are addressed with the words, 'I charge you, therefore, to make confession of your faith, and to answer with all sincerity, and *as in the presence of God*, the questions which I now put to you.' The marriage vow is taken *'in the presence of God* and before these witnesses'. In the solemn moments of life we do make our promise and our pledge in the name and in the presence of God.

It is this kind of thing, a promise made in the name and presence of God, of which the commandment is thinking.

But, when we come to think of it, we can see that every promise is made in the presence of God, whether or not we actually use God's name, for God is everywhere, and God hears every word we say. So what this commandment really means is that, if we make a promise, we must never break it. If we give our word, we must always keep it.

This is not just a religious thing; it is a thing which is necessary in every walk of life and in every transaction between two people. No business deal of any kind would be possible unless we were able to trust people's word. It is like that when millions of pounds are at stake. A shipping firm orders a ship and a shipyard undertakes to make it. The shipyard's owners don't doubt that the people who ordered the ship can and will pay for it, and the people who ordered the ship don't doubt that the shipyard can and will build a ship that is safe and seaworthy. It is that way when much less money is at stake. We leave a pair of shoes to be soled. The cobbler trusts us to pay and we trust him to do the job.

If you look at a Bank of England note, you will see written on it, 'I promise to pay the bearer on demand the sum of one pound.' And it is because we believe that the Bank of England will, if need be, pay, that our bank note is worth a pound. It would be impossible to do business at all, unless people could take each other's word and believe each other's promises.

If promises are as important as that, there are certain things to be said.

i. We should always count the cost of keeping a promise before we make it. One of the most tragic stories in the Bible is about a man who did not do that. His name was Jephthah, and he promised God that, if God would give him the victory in battle, he would sacrifice whatever met him when he came home to his house. Of course, he expected that it would be one of the animals in his farm that met him. But the first person to meet him was his daughter, and to keep his promise he had to sacrifice her (Judges 11:29-40). We now know that God would not want a man to keep a vow like that. But Jephthah was foolish to start with, because he made a promise without thinking out what it might cost.

Jesus always insisted that a man should count the cost. A man once came to him and said that he would like to become his follower. Jesus said to him, 'The foxes have their dens and the birds have their nests, but I haven't got any place to lay my head. Just stop and think of that before you start out to follow me' (Luke 9:57, 58).

There would be no point in setting out to try to be an athlete or a football player unless we were prepared to pay the price in training and in discipline. There would be no point in setting out to be a teacher or a doctor or a scientist, unless we were prepared to pay the price in work and in study. In any undertaking in life we have to count the cost before we start. It is like that with promises. Before we make a promise we should be quite sure that we know what it is going to cost to keep it, and that we are prepared to pay the cost.

ii. Having made the promise, we are bound to keep it. It is little things that show what a man is really like. A man often thinks that what he regards as little things do not matter very much—but they do. There is the kind of man who will promise to meet someone at a certain time, and never turns up at all. There is the kind of man who promises to have something done for a certain time, and never gets it done.

The trouble about that kind of thing is this. If we get into the habit of thinking that what we regard as little and unimportant promises are made to be broken, then we will develop a habit of breaking promises and no one will trust us. There is a proverb which says, 'Sow an act and reap a

habit. Sow a habit and reap a character. Sow a character and
reap a destiny.' A repeated act turns into a habit. Habits
make up character. And character decides destiny.

iii. We could put all this in another way. It is true to say
that the characteristic which is most valued in anyone is
reliability. If an employer is going to employ anyone, his first
question is: Can I trust him? If we are going to be on close
terms with anyone, the first question is: Can I trust him?

Calvin Coolidge was one of the most respected American
Presidents. When he was a boy, he worked on his father's
farm. One day his father and a friend who was staying on
the farm had to be away all day. Before they left in the
morning Calvin's father gave him certain jobs to do. When
his father and the friend came back at night, they had their
meal and settled down. Then the friend said, 'What about
the things you told young Calvin to do? Aren't you going to
check up and see if they're done?' 'I don't need to,' said
Calvin's father. 'If Calvin says he'll do a thing, the thing will be
done.' It was just that quality of reliability that made Calvin
Coolidge the President of the United States of America.
The boy who keeps his promises can reach any height.

Every promise is made in the presence of God, whether
God's name is mentioned or not, and therefore every promise
must be kept. Before we make a promise we should be quite
sure that we are willing to pay the cost of keeping it. Even
the smallest promise is to be kept, for if a man is faithful in
the small things, he will be faithful in the big things, too.
There is no quality in this life so valuable as reliability.

For Discussion

Are there any situations in which people should be released
from their promises?

CHAPTER FIVE

The Special Day

The fourth commandment begins: Remember the Sabbath day to keep it holy (Exodus 20:8.). This is a commandment which we have to look at very carefully indeed, because in one sense it has nothing to do with a Christian at all. As Christians we do not keep the Sabbath any more. The Sabbath is the *last* day of the week; it is our Saturday; and the Jews still keep our Saturday as their Sabbath and as their special day.

Further, we are actually told in the second part of the commandment what the Sabbath commemorates. It commemorates how, as the Old Testament story tells (Genesis 2:2, 3), after he had completed the six days of the work of creation, God rested on the Sabbath day, the seventh day, the last day of the week. For that reason the Sabbath was, in the Jewish law, always to be a day when no one did any work, and when everyone rested, just as God rested on the seventh day. So, according to the Jewish law, you could do no work on the Sabbath. You could not cook a meal, or carry a burden, or write a letter, or kindle a fire, or sew on a button, or even go for a walk. It was a day when God did nothing after the work of creation and when, as the Jews believed, his people must do nothing too.

But the special day which Christians observe is not the Sabbath at all; it is Sunday, or, as it would be better to call it, the Lord's Day. It is not the *last* day of the week; it is the *first* day of the week; and what it commemorates is the Resurrection; it is the day when Jesus rose from the dead. So the Jewish special day is the Sabbath, which is the last

day of the week, and our special day is the Lord's Day, which
is the first day of the week, and the Jewish Sabbath commemorates the day when God rested after the work of the
six days of creation, while the Christian Lord's Day commemorates the day when Jesus rose from the dead. They are
quite different days and they commemorate quite different
things.

We do not quite know when the Christians switched from
the one day to the other, but we do know that before A.D.100
the change had been made, and the Christian Church had
laid it down that we no longer keep the Sabbath but the
Lord's Day. Very likely it came about partly because in the
Roman calendar there was a special day each month called
Sebasté, which means the Emperor's Day. It was a day
specially sacred to the honour of the Roman Emperor; and
the Christians felt that, if the Roman Emperor had a special
day, much more should their Lord Jesus have one. And the
obvious day to choose was the day when the Resurrection
had happened, because for a Christian the Resurrection was
the most important event in the world.

One thing should now be clear. A great deal of the
trouble and controversy about the keeping of the Lord's
Day comes from a confusion between the Jewish Sabbath
and the Christian Lord's Day. Many of the demands that
are made, and many of the rules that are laid down in connection with the Lord's Day are really relevant to the Jewish
Sabbath and not to the Lord's Day at all.

In 18th century Scotland, and in Puritan England, too, the
Sunday was largely a day of prohibitions. It was forbidden
to cook a meal, to set a fire, to shave or to trim the beard.
Water could not be carried; animals could not be foddered;
stalls could not be cleaned; vegetables could not be cut or
gathered from the garden. Even a parson was in trouble for

cooking a shoulder of mutton on the Sunday, and another for powdering his wig on the Sunday. In an account of Sunday in 1704 in Crawford in Lanarkshire, church services went on from 9 o'clock in the morning until 12 o'clock noon; there was then a break and the services continued after an hour's interval until 4 or 5 o'clock in the afternoon. During these times the elders paraded the streets and anyone not at the services was liable to be sternly dealt with. To loiter on the streets, to go for a stroll even after the second service, even 'idly to gaze out of the window' were punishable offences. It is clear that, if there is any justification for this kind of thing at all, it must come from the rigid laws which governed the Jewish Sabbath and not from anything to do with the Christian Lord's Day.

The whole idea of a day when every conceivable action other than religious action is forbidden goes back to the Jewish Sabbath with its insistence on rest rather than to the Christian Lord's Day with its insistence on the joy of the Resurrection.

But all this does not mean that there is no day which is in a special way God's day. There is one word in the commandment which is extremely relevant. Remember the Sabbath day to keep it *holy*. The basic meaning of the word *holy* in Hebrew is *different*. The Temple is holy because it is different from other buildings. The city of Jerusalem is the Holy City because it is different from other cities. The Bible is holy because it is different from other books. There ought to be in the week a day which is different in the sense that it specially belongs to God.

i. The Jewish view is right that there has to be a day of rest. During the French Revolution the revolutionaries, who wished to banish religion, abolished the Sunday. They had to bring it back simply from the health point of view.

The health of the people would not stand having no day of rest.

But two things have to be said about this. First, this is not nearly so relevant now that there is a five day working week and that there is a day of rest from work other than the Sunday. Second, even if there is to be a day of rest, that does not mean that it must be a day of inactivity. The best rest is change of occupation, and for the man who works at a job where he has no exercise at all the best rest would actually be healthy activity. This commandment was first laid down in an agricultural community in which people worked so hard physically that they came to the end of the week physically exhausted, and a day of inactivity was, for them rest. It is not so now. And there is no reason now why a Christian should not engage in health-giving activity in a game or on the road, or at the sea-side, or in the hills on the Lord's Day. There is nothing wrong with physical activity which refreshes a man and makes him fitter for his work.

ii. But there is another and an even more important side to this. We need a different day so that on it we may specially think of God.

The ordinary days of the week are so packed full that we tend to have no time to remember God. That is why it is not nearly enough to think of Sunday in terms of what will refresh the body. It is on Sunday that we think about God and learn about him and come closer to him.

iii. There is one thing left to say. We talk of Sunday being a special day, and in one sense this is true. But in another sense it is true that all days belong equally to God. Therefore, the great use of Sunday is to think about God and learn about God in such a way that it will make a difference to our life and conduct every day of the week. Someone once said that, when he was a child, he always thought of the days of the week as railway carriages and of Sunday as the engine. Sunday is the day which should be the motive power of the whole week. What we do on Sunday should make us live more like true followers of Jesus all through the week, for Sunday is the day when we remember specially that Jesus rose from the dead, and that he is with us always and everywhere.

The Sabbath and the Sunday are not the same. On the Sabbath the Jew remembers how God rested after the six days of creation and on the Sunday the Christian remembers how Jesus rose from the dead. The Sunday is the day that is different. It is meant to give us rest and refreshment, and to do things which relax and strengthen and refresh the body is not wrong. But even more, Sunday is the day on which we remember God. And it is the day when we think about the things that should make us live better and more faithfully every day of the week.

For Discussion

How can we best spend Sunday?

CHAPTER SIX

Honour to Whom Honour is Due

With the fifth commandment we come right home, for the fifth commandment is: Honour your father and your mother (Exodus 20:12). Of all the commandments this should be the easiest to obey.

i. It should be easy to obey this commandment because it is natural to do so. This commandment is, as it were, built into the very structure of life. It is not a commandment which we find only in the Bible. There never was a society of any kind in which this commandment was not accepted as binding. In ancient Greece, for instance, Solon the great law-giver laid it down that, if a son did not support his parents in their old age, when they needed support, he should lose his rights as a citizen. The Greeks believed that to honour parents is part of the basic duty of every citizen of the state. Anyone who has good parents and who does not realise the duty of honouring them is an unnatural person. Nature itself demands that we keep this commandment.

ii. It is a duty of gratitude to keep this commandment. It was our parents who brought us into this world, and we owe them our lives. Of all living creatures man takes longest to become able to support and look after himself.

There is a long time when we cannot get ourselves a home or food or clothes, and when we are entirely dependent on our parents; and there is a considerable part of that time when we are so helpless, that a blow would kill us, and, even if nothing was done to us, and we were just alone, we would certainly die. We ought to find it easy to keep this commandment, if only as a matter of gratitude to those to whom we literally owe the fact that we came into the world, and that we survived through the years when we were quite unable to help ourselves, or to get the things necessary to keep body and soul together.

Apart from that purely physical side of life, many of us owe a great deal to the care and the love and even to the sacrifice of our parents to give us a good start in life. William Soutar the famous Scottish poet said, 'If I have done anything in life, it is because I was able to stand on the shoulders of my father.' It was his father who gave him his chance. We ought to be grateful that in many, many homes the parents do without things and plan and save so that their children should have a chance to do well in life. Of all faults, ingratitude is the ugliest and the most hurting, and not to keep this commandment is to be guilty of ingratitude.

iii. To honour our parents is a matter of common sense. They have walked the journey of life before us, and therefore they know the dangers and the pitfalls in the way. If you are going on a journey through what is to you an unknown country, a map and a guide-book will be very useful, but most useful of all will be the advice and the experience of one who has already travelled that way.

When parents advise their child to do or not to do something, he should understand that it is not because they wish to show their authority or because they are killjoys or because they are old-fashioned, it is because out of their experience they know that the thing is right or wrong, safe or dangerous.

The man who will not listen to the voice of experience will certainly end in trouble—and he will deserve all that is coming to him. Napoleon on one occasion refused to listen to the voice of experience, and his refusal was fatal. He planned to invade Russia. The Russian winters are very severe. He was warned by those who had experience that it was going to be a specially severe winter. They were able to forecast this because on that year the birds had begun to migrate abnormally early, and that was always the sign of a terrible winter to come. Napoleon refused to listen to the advice and the warning. Was he not Napoleon? Ordinary men might need to be careful—not Napoleon. So he went on with his campaign; he was caught in a deadly winter of snow and ice and blizzards. His Grand Army was practically wiped out, and it was for him the beginning of the end—all because he refused to listen to what those who had experience told him. It is sensible to listen to what our parents tell us, because they have an experience of life that we do not yet possess.

But now comes another question—What does it mean to honour our parents? How do we honour them?

i. We honour our parents by loving them and by showing them that we love them. We do not have our parents always; the day will come when they will be taken from this world; and we ought to let them know, while we still have them. We send flowers to a person's funeral as a sign of the respect and affection in which we held him. Someone once said that one gift of flowers given to a person while he is still alive is worth more than a whole cartload of them after he is dead. We should not wait until they are dead to show that we really love our parents.

ii. We honour our parents by doing the things which bring pleasure and pride to them. Nothing pleases parents better than to see their children do well. It may be that a young person is not really very interested in passing examinations and doing well at school or college. Even if he does not care for his own sake, he should care for his parents' sake.

Once a friend of Robert Louis Stevenson found him turning over a scrap-book of press-cuttings which contained all the praises that had been given to him and to his books. 'Well,

Louis,' said the friend, 'is fame all that it's cracked up to be?' Stevenson looked up. 'Yes,' he said, 'when I see my mother's face.' The praise he received might not matter so very much to him, but he did value it when he saw the joy it brought his mother.

Even if you do not care for yourself, remember the joy it brings your parents, when you do well.

There is just one thing left to be said. In life there can be a higher duty than even the duty of honouring our parents. Jesus said, 'He who loves father or mother more than me is not worthy of me' (Matthew 10:37). It will happen rarely, it may well not happen in a life-time, but loyalty to Jesus can clash with the deepest and the greatest loyalties in life.

To take just one example—suppose a young man feels a real call to some job or profession in which he will really be serving Jesus and serving his fellow men. Suppose, for instance, he feels a real call to be a minister. And then suppose his parents, as they think in his own interests, say to him: 'You must go after a better job than that. They don't pay ministers well. You ought to go after a job where you'll make more money and have more social prestige and a better time.' If that happens, the young man has to be true to his call and true to Jesus. When this happens, it is a painful clash. But the last loyalty is to Jesus.

We must honour our parents, because it is natural, because we must show our gratitude, and because it is wise to listen to the voice of experience. We honour them by loving them and by showing it. But the greatest loyalty in the end is to Jesus Christ.

For Discussion

How can we honour our parents?

CHAPTER SEVEN

Life is Sacred

The sixth commandment lays it down: You shall not kill (Exodus 20:13). Whatever this commandment came to mean in the light of Jesus, what it in the first place forbade was murder, and not all killing. It certainly, for instance, did not mean that there cannot be the infliction of the death penalty for a crime, for in this chapter and in the next there are listed many breaches of the law which are punishable by death (Exodus 21:12-14, 15, 16, 17, 29; 22:19, 20). What is forbidden by the commandment is the reckless taking of life by any individual in anger, in violence or in bitterness, in uncontrolled passion, for vengeance or for robbery or for any selfish purpose; but it does not, as first laid down, forbid the judicial killing of a man because he has committed some crime against society or because he has broken certain of the great and serious laws which society has laid down. But it is also true that it has necessary implications and ramifications which are of very great importance.

i. About the killing which is murder we do not need to argue. There is no need to try to prove that that kind of killing is wrong. To kill a man in anger, to kill a man in order to eliminate him so that some thing or some person may be gained, to kill in violence in the process of robbery, does not need to be proved wrong. That is something which everyone accepts as wrong, and it is something which must always be wrong, if life is to go on at all in any kind of order and security.

ii. But there are other ways in which a man may be said to be killed. In the twentieth century the law lays it down that working conditions must be safe and that they must not be injurious or poisonous to the workman; but it was not always so. There was a time—and not so very long ago— when a coal-miner's expectation of life was less than forty years because of the damage done to his lungs by the coal dust in the pits. Less than a hundred years ago one of the most poisonous trades was that of making matches. Matches were dipped in phosphorus and phosphorus is a highly corrosive substance. It literally ate away the fingers of the workers. It ate into their faces until the very jaw-bones were laid bare. If the light was put out in a room in which matches were being tipped, you could see the hands and jaws of the workers gleam with the phosphorescent light as the phosphorus ate away their very flesh.

To employ men and women in circumstances like that was to kill them. That kind of thing does not happen now. Laws have been made to see that it is impossible. But what are we to say of the explosions of nuclear weapons, for instance? Where such weapons are exploded, there is radiation in the air. It is claimed that the radiation is not enough to do damage; but it is also true that an increasing number of children are born dreadfully deformed and there is an increasing number of cases of leukaemia, which is cancer of the blood; and it may well be that this is due to radiation in the air. We may well as Christians still have to fight against things which kill people—and such killing is a kind of murder.

iii. In the nineteenth century thousands of people were compelled to live under conditions which in the end killed them. As many as a dozen or fourteen lived in a single room; there was no ventilation; water was bad and cholera raged; it was quite common for fourteen families to share one lavatory. The result was that killer diseases like tuberculosis and diphtheria were rife, and people died by the thousand.

To compel people to live in conditions like that was equivalent to killing them. This is something which is by no means ended even yet. It is to the shame of the Church that in the nineteenth century the Church did not protest about these things. Today it is still a Christian duty to do everything to see that people are not compelled to live in conditions which can kill or maim them.

iv. In the middle of the twentieth century there is a new phenomenon. This is the widespread use of drugs which can be killers. There are drugs which are so habit-forming that the taker in the end becomes unable to retain his sanity, and these drugs slowly destroy him both physically and mentally. Someone has to sell these drugs; and to sell them is to be nothing other than a partner in murder. We should always refuse to have anything to do with them.

v. There is one other form of killing in which any of us might be involved, that is the killing in war. Every person has to settle for himself the question: Can a Christian go to war?

On the one hand, it is argued that the most precious things in life have to be defended; it is argued that the Christian cannot stand by and see evil rampant and unchecked. There are few, if any, who would say that a war of aggression is ever justified, but there are many who would say that sometimes, if only rarely, a war of defence is a Christian duty, if Christianity itself is to be defended.

This is something which each of us must decide for himself. But it is my own conviction that a Christian cannot go to war. Very briefly, I set out reasons.

i. It is the teaching of Jesus that we should love our enemies, and no one can love a man by killing him.

ii. It is the Christian teaching that all punishment must

be designed for the reformation of the wrong-doer, and we can never reform anyone by blasting him out of existence.

iii. Christianity does not say that evil must go unchecked. It would be quite right to stop someone who was attacking a weaker person or assaulting someone we love; but in that case it is the actual person who does the wrong who is being stopped, if need be, by force, whereas in war a nuclear bomb can destroy tens of thousands of quite innocent people completely indiscriminately, and can mutilate for life babies still unborn. It does not seem to me that indiscriminate slaughter like that can ever be justified. To put it maybe over-simply, but there is no other test, can you imagine Jesus pressing the button which would release a nuclear bomb?

iv. It is argued that unless war is waged, the finest values might be destroyed and perhaps even Christianity itself. But this argument involves arguing that it is right to preserve what is good by doing what is wrong; and, if we believe that Christianity is from God, then we ought also to believe that Christianity, even if it has to suffer terribly, can and must ultimately triumph, because it is indestructible.

v. Finally, we have the example of Jesus himself. With his powers he could have blasted his enemies out of existence —but he chose the Cross, and it may be that his followers must do the same.

To kill is wrong. To make people work or live under conditions which will kill them is to break the commandment. To traffic in drugs is as bad as to kill. The Christian must himself decide whether or not war is always wrong for him.

For Discussion

Can a Christian engage in war? What should the Christian's attitude be to authority?

CHAPTER EIGHT

The Essential Purity

The seventh commandment is, You shall not commit adultery (Exodus 20:14). In the second half of the twentieth century and in the kind of society in which we are living this is a commandment which it is essential to face. The New Testament is insistent on two things.

i. The New Testament is insistent on the essential character of purity. 'Shun immorality,' Paul writes (I Corinthians 6:18). Immorality and impurity are not even to be named, much less practised, by Christians (Ephesians 5:3-18). All immorality and impurity and uncontrolled passion are to be put to death, for these things bring upon us the wrath of God (Colossians 3:5-6). The New Testament insists that purity and Christianity go hand in hand.

ii. The New Testament is insistent that our bodies as well as our souls belong to God, and that we cannot and must not do what we like with them. We are to present our bodies as a living sacrifice to God (Romans 12:1). Our bodies can and ought to be the dwelling-place of the Holy Spirit (I Corinthians 3:16; 6:19). Christianity never did teach that the soul is so important that it does not matter what we do with our bodies; it has always taught that our bodies belong to God and we must use them as he would have us use them.

Before we go on to discuss the significance of this commandment for us we must note one technical matter of words. Adultery is sexual intercourse with another person who is married; fornication is sexual intercourse before marriage. And, of course, both are equally condemned.

In ancient Greece and Rome people saw nothing wrong in

having sexual intercourse before they were married and out-side marriage. It brought no stigma and no moral condemnation; it was part and parcel of the ordinary way of life and living. When Christianity came, it taught that sexual intercourse is part of the life-long marriage bond. But we are living today in a society in which a great many people see no harm in having sexual relationships before they are married. It may well be that we know friends who are like this; and we may ask, If other people do it, why should we not do it? Why should we have to be different? We are going to look at these questions.

i. We can begin with something which is a general truth, and which is very important, because it tends to be forgotten. *The hall-mark of a real man is self-control and self-discipline.* It is exactly here that there is one of the essential differences between a man and an animal. An animal has no self-control and will satisfy its desires whenever these desires arise. A man is a creature who can control and discipline himself. To allow our sexual passions to master us is to allow the animal part of us to be supreme, and to allow the part of us that is true manhood to be defeated.

Sometimes you will be told that it is manly to do these things; but it is the reverse of manly, it is animal. True manhood means self-control.

ii. To have sexual intercourse before marriage is to demand the privileges of life without accepting the duties and the responsibilities of life. To have sexual intercourse together is one of the biggest privileges that two people can have, for in that act they give themselves to each other. But that privilege should not be claimed and enjoyed until after the two people have accepted the responsibility of setting up a house and a home and rearing a family. Otherwise it is to want to take everything and to give nothing. It is to be irresponsible, and there are few sins which cause more disasters than irresponsibility.

iii. Sexual intercourse should be the consummation of the relationship between two people. The Bible speaks of two people *knowing* each other when it means that they have had sexual intercourse with each other. 'Adam *knew* Eve his wife, and she conceived and bore Cain' (Genesis 4:1). This is something which should happen only when two people know each other completely and altogether. It is not something which should happen when two people are almost strangers; it should never be a thing done in the passing. It is and was meant to be something which comes at the end of a relationship in which two people come to know each other so well that they decide to share, not just that act, but all life together.

iv. One of the arguments is that if two people love each other and intend to get married, why should they wait until they are married to have sexual intercourse together? There are two answers to that.

(*a*) One is very practical. It is that, however much two people intend to get married, life is an uncertain business. Even the closest relationship can somehow come unstuck. In this kind of thing there is no such thing as absolute certainty.

(*b*) The second is much more important. If you really love a person, the last thing that you will ever want is to do anything which has the slightest chance of hurting that person. Now the plain fact is that, if you have sexual intercourse, there may be a baby. With all the precautions in the world that may happen. And, if it does you have deeply hurt the life of the person you claim to love, and you have brought into this world a child who starts with the handicap of being illegitimate.

Really to love a person is not a reason for sexual intercourse before marriage; it is by far the strongest argument against it.

v. There is something else to be said. If two people have sexual intercourse before they are married, they will almost certainly have to do so in circumstances of concealment and of anxiety and of haste. The whole action is spoiled. That which should give deep satisfaction becomes something which is done hurriedly and nervously and in the wrong way altogether. From the beginning the circumstances are the reverse of what they ought to be.

vi. Lastly, it is the simple truth that, when it comes to marriage, almost everyone would wish to marry someone who has not given himself or herself to someone else. A person like that is far more likely to be a good partner in life than a person who has let passion be his ruler.

There remain certain very practical things to be said. This purity, this self-control, is not always easy. We should never do things which make it more difficult. For instance, alcohol slackens self-control, and the wise person will avoid it. Moreover the man with self-control will know at what point he must stop. His conscience will tell him the point at which he must go no further, and he will not allow himself to engage in the kind of petting which can be the way to trouble.

We are living in an age today when purity is sometimes laughed at. We should remember that our bodies, too, belong to God. We should remember that self-control is the test of true manhood. We should not claim privilege without responsibility. We should not hasten to take that which ought only to come at the end of a long relationship. We should remember that true love will never do anything that should hurt or harm another. We should not degrade a beautiful act by doing it in a secretive and anxious way. We should remember that loyalty matters before anything else. We should not do the things that make self-control difficult. And above all we should remember the presence of Jesus, and do nothing we would not wish him to see.

For Discussion

Why is chastity so important?

CHAPTER NINE

Things We Have no Right to Take

The eighth commandment is: You shall not steal (Exodus 20:15). This is simply to say that we must never take what we have no right to take.

We might say of stealing that it is a 'natural' sin. It is human nature to want what we have not got; and the desire may turn to action; and, when it does, a man may steal. We do not need to argue about the rightness of this commandment. Everyone agrees that stealing is wrong.

We are all agreed that, for instance, to steal money is wrong and to burgle a shop or a bank is wrong, and on the whole we are not likely to be involved in this kind of stealing. But there is in society today a kind of stealing which is considered to be clever rather than blameworthy.

i. First, then, let us look at the kind of stealing in which some people almost take a pride.

Here are three typical examples. There is travelling by bus, or rail without paying the fare. Again and again, when sudden checks are made, we find the most respectable people, and people who have no need at all to do it, guilty of this kind of thing. There is stealing in the super-market type of shop, where everything is laid out and there are no shop assistants. Here also we find otherwise respectable people, who are by no means poor, guilty of stealing. There is pilfering at work. One of the problems in the factories and in the yards just now is the amount of pilfering that goes on. There are people who think it rather clever to cheat the bus company or the railway, to evade the shop detective, to smuggle things out of the place in which they work.

To put it plainly, no matter whom or where we take things from, if we have no right to take them, it is stealing. We may not like to be told so, but if we do these things we are just thieves. To do things like that is not clever; it is dishonest.

ii. There is the kind of stealing that goes on in a game. The most desirable thing used to be *sportsmanship;* nowadays we are in danger of regarding *gamesmanship* as the most desirable thing. In gamesmanship a player resorts to all kinds of dishonest tactics to win. You find players claiming things which they know quite well are wrong; a player, for instance, claiming a corner when he knows it is a goal-kick; a player protesting at a foul given against him when he knows that he is guilty. Games are being ruined because too many players try to cheat the referee. That kind of thing is not clever; it is just cheating; it is claiming what we have no right to have. And, so far from pleasing the spectators, it disgusts them.

iii. There is another kind of stealing of which a great many of us are too often guilty, and that is the stealing of time. When we start a job, we enter into a contract with the person for whom we work. The contract is that we work for so many hours and the employer gives us so much money in return. This is to say that within these hours our time belongs to our employer, because he has paid for it. We would be very annoyed if he did not keep his part of the bargain. But we too have a duty. To waste time, to idle when we should be working, to start late and to stop early, is to steal time for which we have been paid.

A great many of our industrial problems would be solved, if employer and employee alike kept the bargain which they had made with each other.

When we think of these things, it becomes clear that, even if we would never pick a pocket, or rob a bank, or burgle a shop, we can nevertheless be guilty of stealing. How can we avoid this?

i. There was in Greece a very wise philosopher called Epicurus. He said that the greatest good in life is pleasure. A great many people thought that he was just giving them a licence to do as they liked. But he did not leave the matter there. He went on to say that you have to take the long view of pleasure. You have to ask, not how the thing feels at the moment, but how it will feel in the days to come. And, he went on to say, when you look at it like that, the only way to be happy is to be good. He took the example of this very thing, of stealing. At the moment you steal, you may think that this is great; you have got what you think you want. But, he said, for ever after you are left with the continual fear that you may be found out, and, in the long run you have got yourself unhappiness and not happiness.

No one can be happy if he steals, because, whether he likes it or not, he will find it coming into his memory and giving him a twinge of fear. If we want to be happy we have got to be honest; that is the law of life.

ii. There is another way of putting this. Can you really live with yourself, if you know that you are a thief? We can lose almost everything and still get along in life; but there is one thing we cannot lose and still find life liveable, and that is our self-respect. And we cannot know that we are dishonest and respect ourselves.

iii. When we are thinking of life and conduct, we always in the end come back to the same thing. We have to remember that God sees our every action and hears our every word, and therefore we must make life fit for him to see—and no one would want God to see him do a dishonest thing.

We would all agree that stealing is wrong and we would all condemn the man who is a thief. But we have to be careful

that we ourselves never steal. We must never take a pride in
the dishonesty that tries to get away with wrong things. We
must be above petty theft and pilfering. We must play
games absolutely fairly. We must remember that it is possible
to steal time as well as things. We must remember that, if we
steal, fear enters into life and self-respect leaves it. And we
must never do things which it would grieve God to see.

For Discussion

What forms of dishonesty is it easy to practise at our work?

CHAPTER TEN

Nothing but the Truth

The ninth commandment says: You shall not bear false witness against your neighbour (Exodus 20:16; Deuteronomy 5:20). In the beginning this had to do with the law-courts, and lays it down that when a man is giving evidence about anyone that evidence must be true.

The Jews had a horror of false witness and condemned wholeheartedly the man who did not speak the truth. 'A faithful witness does not lie, but a false witness breathes out lies' (Proverbs 14:5) 'A false witness will not go unpunished, and he who utters lies will not escape' (Proverbs 19:5). They believed that a man who tells lies about other people will not go unpunished by God.

More than once the Jewish law insists that no man can be condemned on the evidence of one witness; there must always be two or three witnesses and their stories must agree (Deuteronomy 19:16-19; Numbers 35:30). The law lays down what must be done (Deuteronomy 19:16-19). If there is any suspicion that a witness is malicious and false, he is to be examined. If he is found to have been a false witness, the same penalty as he tried to inflict on the person against whom he gave his false evidence, is to be inflicted upon him.

But this has to do with much more than giving evidence in a court of law. There we will have to swear that on this particular occasion we will tell the truth, the whole truth, and nothing but the truth. This commandment has to do with telling the truth all the time. The Jewish law said; 'You shall not utter a false report' (Exodus 23:1). This commandment means that we must speak the truth at all times, and not just in a law-court. That being so, certain things have to be recognized.

i. When we think of it, it is by no means easy to tell the truth. Two people can give an account of the same incident, and the accounts turn out quite different. For instance, two people may give an account of the same game of football, and you would not know that it was the same game that they were talking about. Two people could describe the same player; one might call him an enthusiastic player and the other might call him a dirty player.

It is the same, for instance, with an accident on the road. Two drivers involved in an accident might each tell the story in a way which puts the blame on the other. After hearing the evidence in a case like that a judge once said that, if you were to believe the evidence of both sides, there was a head-on collision between two cars, each of which was stationary on its own side of the road!

(a) We need to get rid of prejudice. If we are prejudiced in a person's favour, that person can do no wrong; if we are prejudiced against him, that person can do no right. Prejudice blinds any man to the truth. We must always ask ourselves: Am I really being fair?

(b) We need to get rid of self-interest. We are very apt to tell a story in such a way that we come out of it well. We tell it to put ourselves in the best possible light.

(c) We need to get rid of self-protection. In telling any story, we are very apt to put the blame on the other person. We are often, even if unconsciously, afraid to tell the truth.

ii. The other side of this is that it is easy to slip into inaccuracy. Dr. Johnson used to say that from his earliest years a child should be compelled to be absolutely truthful, and even if he said that he saw a thing out of one window when he in fact saw it out of another, he should be pulled up.

Dr. Johnson insisted that we should build up the habit of absolute accuracy in statement.

We all know how easy it is, for instance, to exaggerate, how easy it is to make statements which are not quite true, how easy it is to make excuses which twist the truth just a little to suit ourselves and to protect ourselves.

It is well to remember that it takes a real effort to be strictly accurate.

iii. A third thing to remember is that it is extremely dangerous not to tell the truth. We saw that one of the things that the Bible says is, 'You shall not utter a false report' (Exodus 23:1). One of our commonest faults is repeating stories about other people, and the odd thing is that we usually take more pleasure in telling a story to someone's discredit than to his credit.

By repeating gossip it is possible to ruin a person's character. Iago, in Shakespeare's play *Othello*, says:

> 'Who steals my purse steals trash. . . .
> But he who filches from me my good name. . . .
> . . . . makes me poor indeed.'

Never repeat a story about someone else, unless you know that it is true, and never repeat it even then if it is going to damage that person's good name and reputation. The trouble about a word is that you cannot get it back once it is spoken and it may go on and on doing all kinds of damage. Few things do more harm than gossip.

iv. When we speak about telling the truth, one special point arises. Must we always tell the truth baldly and bluntly? For instance, if a person has played a game or sung a song or given some kind of performance, and not done very well, must we say that he was no good, or is there any harm in the polite compliment which will encourage him, even if it is not strictly true? Must we tell the truth, even when it is unpleasant and when it might hurt?

Someone has given us a valuable rule about this. There are three questions we should always ask about anything we say about anyone else, or to anyone else. The first question is: *Is it true*? And, of course, if it is not true, then it must not be said at all. The second question is: *Is it necessary*? If it is necessary, it will have to be said, but there are not many times when politeness and courtesy need to be disregarded. The third question is: *Is it kind*? It is hardly ever a duty to be unkind. There are ways and ways of telling the truth. You can tell it in a way that is deliberately designed to wound and hurt; there are people who take a delight in seeing other people wince when something is said. On the other hand, it was said of Florence Allshorn, a great teacher, that, when she had some criticism to make, she always made it, as it were, with her arm round your shoulder. She spoke the truth; she said what was necessary; but she took care to say it kindly and in a way that would help and not hurt. And that is the best rule of all.

There is one thing which should make us specially careful about our words. Jesus said, 'I tell you, on the day of judgment men will render account for every careless word they utter' (Matthew 12:36).

The truth must be told. It is not easy to tell the truth; it is easy to slip into a lie; so we must always be on the watch. We must never repeat the gossip that will hurt someone else's reputation. Before we say anything we must ask if it is true, and necessary, and kind. And above all we must remember that we will answer to God for all we say.

For Discussion

In what ways do we give our tongues too much licence?

CHAPTER ELEVEN

The Forbidden Desire

The tenth and last commandment is: You shall not covet (Exodus 20:17). This is a different kind of commandment from any of the others. The others deal with a man's actions; they forbid him to kill, to steal, to commit adultery, to bear false witness. They order him to keep the Sabbath and to honour his father and mother. They insist that he must worship only the one true God, and that he must never make a graven image. All these things are matters of action. But this last commandment deals, not with a man's actions, but with his thoughts and his desires. That is why it is by far the most searching and the most far-reaching of the commandments. We can control our actions; but it is another matter to control our thoughts and our desires. We can, for instance, stop ourselves stealing, but it is a different thing to stop ourselves *wanting* to steal. We can stop ourselves hitting another man; but it is a different thing to stop ourselves *wanting* to hit him. Outward actions can be controlled; inward thoughts and desires are far more difficult to control. This is far and away the most difficult commandment to obey.

We begin by noting an important fact. We could call the word *covet* a neutral word, because it can be used, and is used, in the New Testament, in two senses. It is used in a bad sense, the sense in which covetousness, is altogether forbidden. But Paul also, as the Authorised Version has it, tells his people to covet to prophesy (I Corinthians 14:39) and to covet earnestly the best gifts (I Corinthians 12:31). There is a way of coveting which is bad, and a way of coveting which is good.

The reason for this is in the meaning of the word itself. To covet means *to desire earnestly*, to long for; and we can earnestly desire the things we need to make life fine and good. The first kind of covetousness is bad; the second kind is a necessary ingredient in the good life.

It is, of course, with the bad covetousness that the commandment is concerned. The minds of most people have an odd characteristic. Once a thing is forbidden, it tends to become attractive. We tend almost instinctively to want what we are told we must not have. The great saint Augustine tells how, when he was a boy, he and his friends made a raid on a garden and stole some pears. He had far better pears in his own garden, he says. The pears they stole were so hard and sour they could not eat them. The sole pleasure they got was the pleasure of the raid, the pleasure of getting that which was forbidden. To want what is forbidden happens to nearly everyone. We have to be on guard not to allow ourselves to want to do things simply for the kick of doing what is forbidden.

What this commandment really says is that we ought to be content with what we have. Contentment comes from inside of us, not from outside. If a person has a discontented nature, he could get the sun and the moon and the stars and still be discontented. The ancient Stoics had a wise saying: 'If you want to make a man happy, add not to his possessions, but take away from his desires'. All the things in the world will not make a naturally discontented person contented. The secret of contentment is within us.

We talked of how natural it is to desire the thing which is forbidden. It is also natural to desire what other people have. The odd thing thus is that we covet the kind of life someone else lives and he covets the kind of life that we live. A poor man might envy a rich man for his money, and a rich man might envy the same poor man for his health. A tradesman might envy a parson or a doctor or a university teacher for the kind of life that they live; while they might envy him because he works from 9 until 5.30 and then stops. It always seems that the other man is better off than we are. A very old story puts this into a kind of parable. It is called the House with the Golden Windows. There was a boy who lived in a house on one side of a valley. On the other side of the valley there was another house, which he saw every day, but which he had never visited. To him it was the most wonderful house in the world, for when he looked at it every morning it seemed to have windows of gold, and he always called it the House with the Golden Windows. One day he decided to visit it. He took a picnic lunch and he started out to walk across the valley. At last he reached the house on the other side. At the door there was a boy about his own age. This other boy spoke to him: 'Where do you come from?' The boy said, 'I come from that house that you can see across the valley.' And the *other* boy said at once, 'You're the boy that lives in the House with the Golden Windows. Every evening I see the windows of your house pure gold.' 'But no', said the first boy, '*you* are the one that lives in the House with the Golden Windows.' 'I'm not,' said the second boy, 'it's you who lives there.' By this time it was evening. 'Look,' said the second boy, 'you can see it for yourself. Look! There's your house and the windows are gold.'

Of course, what really happened was this. In the morning the sun shone on the house on one side of the valley, so that it looked as if it had golden windows. In the evening the sun shone on the house on the other side of the valley, so that it now seemed to have golden windows. Each boy thought that the other boy's house had golden windows.

We always think that the other person's life is better than ours.

But there is one thing we must always say. We must say, 'God made me as I am, and God put me where I am, and God has something he wants me to do just as I am right here.' Our job is not to envy someone else's life, but to make the very best of our own.

There is another side to this. This other side is not in the commandment, but has to be taken along with it. The commandment tells us that we have to be content with *what we have*, but we must never be content with *what we are*— not in the sense of the kind of job we have got, but in the sense of the kind of person we are. That is where the right kind of covetousness comes in. We must always covet the knowledge and the goodness, the mind and the character, which so far we have not got. The example of Jesus is always before us, and we must always be trying our hardest to get closer and closer to it. It is right to say, 'I wish I was like that,' and it is right to do everything we can to be like that.

To covet something is earnestly to desire it. We have always to be on the watch against covetousness, because, when a thing is forbidden, it tends at once to become attractive. Our task in life is not to covet what others have, but to do the best we can where we are and with what we have. But, as there is a wrong covetousness, so there is a right covetousness, and as there is a right kind of contentment, so there is a wrong kind of contentment. It is right to be content with what we have; it is never right to be content with what we are. All our lives we should be earnestly desiring to be more like Jesus, and with his help, always trying our hardest to be so.

For Discussion

What sort of things ought we to covet?

THE NEW LAW

We have studied the Ten Commandments. They are not specially and characteristically Christian. Men knew them thousands of years before Jesus came into the world. They have not been abandoned and left behind; they are still valid. They are the principles by which all good men live, not the particular principles by which a Christian lives.

We might call the Ten Commandments *the old law*; but we have *a new law* as well, which came with Jesus. The *new law* goes far beyond the old law, and is the law by which the Christian lives. This new law is to be found especially in the Sermon on the Mount, in which we have the teaching which is uniquely the teaching of Jesus.

It is the Sermon on the Mount that we are now going to study.

CHAPTER TWELVE

The Description of the Christian

Matthew 5.1-11

There are eight Beatitudes, but the Beatitudes are not the description of eight different people; they are the description of one person. The Beatitudes are the description of the character of the Christian and they fall into three sections.

i. Three of them deal with *the beginning of the Christian life*.

(*a*) First, there is: Blessed are the poor in spirit. The word which is used for *poor* does not just mean *poor*; it means *destitute*. It describes, not the man who has not enough but the man who has nothing at all.

This word for *poor* has a special use in the Old Testament. First of all, it describes the man who is simply poor. Then it goes on to describe the man who, because he is poor, has no influence and no standing, and who is downtrodden and oppressed. Then finally it goes on to describe the man who, because he has no one on earth to help him, has put his whole trust in God.

What this Beatitude says is: Happy is the man who has realized that he has absolutely nothing of his own and who has put his whole trust in God.

There are a great many things that we can get only when we are prepared to admit that we need them. If we are ill, we cannot be cured, until we admit that we are ill and go to see a doctor. If we do not know something, we cannot learn about it, until we admit our ignorance and go to the expert who can teach us.

The first thing necessary in life is to admit that we cannot live it well by ourselves, and that we need God's help. If we try to face our temptations by ourselves, we fall to them. If we try to make our decisions by ourselves, we often make the wrong ones. If we try to do by ourselves the difficult things we have to do, we often fail to do them.

Abraham Lincoln said that he would be the biggest fool on earth if he thought he could carry out the duties of the presidency for one day without the help of One who was greater and wiser and stronger than he.

The first thing we need in the Christian life is to realize and to admit that we need the help of Jesus.

(b) Second, there is: Blessed are those who mourn. To mourn is to be sorry. This Beatitude means: Happy is the man who is sorry for the wrong things that he has done.

There are people who boast about the wrong things they have done; they think it clever to break the law and to do things which are forbidden. There are people who do wrong things and are sorry if they are found out, but who would do exactly the same again, if they thought that they would get away with it.

Every time we do a wrong thing we hurt and worry those who love us and we hurt and worry God. John Masefield tells of a man whose first step towards becoming a Christian was the discovery of 'the harm I've done by being me'.

We have to be really sorry for all the wrong things that we have done.

(c) Third, there is: Blessed are those who hunger and thirst for righteousness. Most of us have never really known what it is to be really starving and really in danger of dying of thirst. The people Jesus spoke to did know. In Palestine in the time of Jesus a working man's wage was 4p a day. People ate meat at the most only once a week. If a man was unemployed for two or three days he and his family would be literally starving. In the East there is the hot wind and the sandstorm. If a man was caught without water out in the desert, he could die of thirst. We have simply to turn a tap in our homes and the water flows; in the East people went about the street selling water.

What this Beatitude means is: Happy is the man who wants goodness as much as a starving man wants bread, and as much as a man dying of thirst wants water. So the third step in the Christian life is to want goodness like that.

If we want a thing enough, we usually manage to get it. Often we are not good for the simple reason that we do not want it enough. We should want goodness as much as the man dying of hunger and thirst wants food and water. And one way to get that desire is to remember that to be good is the only way to bring happiness to those who love us and happiness to God.

So the Christian life starts with three things—realizing that we need the help of Jesus, really being sorry for the wrong things we have done, and wanting goodness more than anything else in the world.

ii. Four of the Beatitudes deal with *what the Christian man is*.

(a) First, there is: Blessed are the meek. This word *meek* is very hard to put into modern English. Aristotle wrote a great deal about this quality. He described every virtue as the happy medium between two opposite extremes. So on the one hand you have the spendthrift, and on the other hand you have the miser, and in between the properly generous man. On the one hand you have the reckless man, on the other hand you have the coward, and in between the really brave man.

So he said that this quality of meekness describes the happy medium between too much and too little anger. It describes the man who is angry for the right reasons, in the right way, at the right things and for the right length of time. So what this Beatitude says is: Happy is the man who is always angry at the right time and never at the wrong time. The Christian has such perfect control of himself with the help of Jesus that he is always angry when it is right to be angry and never angry when it is wrong to be angry.

(b) There is: Blessed are the merciful. At first sight in English this looks as if it means just that it is the Christian thing to be kind. But the word that is used for *merciful* is a wonderful word. It describes the person who can so put himself in the place of others that he can think with their mind and feel with their heart. It is the ability to get right inside other people so that we can think and feel as they do.

This is not easy. We are usually so concerned with our own feelings that we never bother about other people's feelings. But a Christian must be just as much, and even more, concerned with other people's feelings as with his own. To take just one example, it will make it very much easier to forgive people for what they have done, if we really try to enter into their minds and to understand why they did it.

(c) There is: Blessed are the pure in heart. The word used for *pure* is very interesting. We can see what it means if we see how it is used. It is used for grain that is mixed with no chaff, for wine that is mixed with no water, for metal that is mixed with no alloy, for a style that is mixed with no grammatical faults, for an army which has no cowards in it. It always has this idea of something unmixed with any inferior thing.

What this really means is: Blessed are those whose motives are absolutely unmixed, those who do things for nothing but the right reasons.

For instance, if we help someone, is our motive only to help, or do we do it to feel pleased with ourselves?

The Christian is a person who does things for nothing but the right reasons.

(d) There is: Blessed are the peacemakers. The thing we have to note here is that it is the peace *makers* who are blessed, not necessarily the peace *lovers*.

It sometimes happens that there is a bad situation in a group or in a committee and everyone knows it. But instead of doing something about it, people say, 'Let it alone for peace's sake.' That is not the way to peace; that is the way to trouble. The kind of peace this Beatitude speaks of is not the peace that comes from running away from things, but the peace that comes from facing them.

What, then, is this peace? It means *right relations between people*. What this Beatitude says is: Happy is the man who helps people to be friends. And if that kind of man is blessed, we must always remember that this means that the trouble-maker is condemned. The Christian always helps people to be friends and never causes trouble between them.

So the Christian is a man who is always angry at the right time and never at the wrong time, a man who always tries to understand how others feel, a man who always acts for nothing but the right reasons, and a man whose influence makes people friends with each other.

iii. One of the Beatitudes deals with *the result of the Christian life*.

This is: Blessed are those who are persecuted for right-eousness' sake. The Christian has to be prepared to suffer for his beliefs.

The Christian is different and he must never be ashamed or afraid to be different. He has to be honest and he has to be pure and he has to be kind. He has to insist that he must do certain things and he has also absolutely to refuse to do certain other things.

But the Christian will always remember that, when he has to suffer something for Jesus sake, Jesus too suffered. And it is true that where there is no cross, there is no crown.

For Discussion

In what ways may a Christian have to suffer because of his faith?

C

CHAPTER THIRTEEN

The Salt of the Earth

Matthew 5:13

To this day when we want to describe a specially fine person, we say, 'People like that are the salt of the earth.' This is what Jesus said that a Christian ought to be. What did He mean when He said, 'You are the salt of the earth'? In the ancient world people connected salt with three things.

i. They connected salt with *usefulness*. 'There is nothing more useful,' they said, 'than sun and salt.' So then a characteristic of the Christian is that he is useful.

This is something that everyone can be. We cannot all be brilliant, but we can all be useful.

A famous author tells a story of his boyhood. It was in the days when a boy started with as little as two shillings a week. He got his first pay and took it home and gave it to his mother. The next day they were sitting at their evening meal. On the table there was a loaf still uncut. As the meal began, the mother took the knife and began to slice the loaf. Then she looked up. 'Johnnie,' she said, 'it was you who bought that loaf for us.' It was her way of telling him that he had become a real contributor to the home and to the family. And he tells us that, even after he had become wealthy and famous, he never again had a moment which made him feel as proud. We should be proud to be of use.

ii. They connected salt with *flavour*. Everyone knows how tasteless food can be without salt. It is salt which adds flavour to things.

So the Christian ought to add flavour to life. Too often people think of a Christian as a gloomy person who disapproves of everything and of everyone; and unfortunately there are Christians like that. But if you read descriptions of heaven in the Bible, you get the impression that heaven is a place full of music where people sing together for joy.

The Christian should be a person who is happy himself, and who makes others happy.

It has been claimed that it is medically true that the people who laugh most live longest. Laughter is good for us because it expands the lungs and lets fresh air into the body! So then we can even say that laughter is a life-giving tonic.

iii. They connected salt with *preservation*. They had no refrigerators in the ancient world; they could not make artificial ice and pack things in it; they could not pack things in air-tight containers. Salt was the only thing they knew that could keep things fresh and preserve them from going bad. Salt, they said, can put life even into a dead body.

Salt was the great preservative to keep things from going bad. The Christian should be like that. He should be like a conscience to any group in which he happens to be, always ready to protest against anything that is low and impure.

We all know that there are certain people to whom it is easy to tell a smutty story, and certain others to whom you would never dream of saying anything soiled or impure. We all know that there are certain people who bring down the tone of any group into which they enter, and that there are certain others who lift it up. The Christian should be the kind of person who carries with him an atmosphere in which nothing soiled or impure can live.

We have to be the salt of the earth. Wherever we are, we must be useful. Wherever we are, we must bring flavour into life. Wherever we are, we have to be the influence which keeps words and actions clean.

For Discussion

How can a person be an influence for good at his work?

CHAPTER FOURTEEN

Lights of the World

Matthew 5:14-16

After Jesus had said that the Christians must be the salt of the earth, he went on to say they must be the light of the world. Let us see what He meant by that.

i. The most obvious thing about a light is that *it can be seen*. A light is meant to be seen, not to be hidden. It is like a city that stands on a hilltop; everyone can see it.

This means that everyone must be able to see that we are Christians. It is natural to be proud to show what side you are on and what country you belong to. When we go to a cup-tie or to an international match, we are proud to wear our club's or our country's colours.

We should feel the same about being a Christian. Twice Paul insisted that he was not ashamed of the Gospel and that he was not ashamed to show that he was a follower of Jesus (Romans 1:16, 2 Timothy 1:12).

No one can really be a secret disciple, for as Richard Glover said, the secrecy either kills the discipleship, or the discipleship kills the secrecy. And to show that we are followers of Jesus does not mean going about looking specially holy, or carrying an outsize Bible. It means anywhere and in any company doing what we know Jesus would want us to do, and refusing to do what we know he would not want us to do.

ii. A light has more than one use. A light is a guide. It is very much easier to find your way when there is a light. In the Underground in London they have a system of different lights for the different railway lines, and you follow the right colour of light to get the line on which you want to travel.

If a light is a guide, and if we have to be a light, this means that we must be an example to other people. Again and again people are waiting for a lead. If someone stands up and gives them an example, they will do the right thing. But they need the lead and the example.

I remember when we were at school some of us once played truant for an hour or two. We were duly carpeted. The first three or four boys made the lamest excuses. Then one boy said: 'Sir, I have no excuse', and after that no one else made any lame excuses; everyone honestly admitted he was wrong. If we do the right thing, we will find that we do not have to do it alone. There are others who are only waiting for an example and they will follow.

iii. Quite often a light can be a *warning*. The traffic lights are warnings; the red light on level-crossing gates is a warning; there are lights to tell us what streets are one-way streets. A light can often be the means of stopping us taking some wrong turning or some wrong road.

In this way, too, we must be a light. If we see someone doing the wrong things, or behaving in a way that is likely to get him into trouble and even to spoil his whole life, it is our duty to try to stop him. It would be a very sad thing if later in life someone was to come to us and say, 'I would never have made such a mess of things, if only you had warned me.'

This is not an easy thing to do, and if we do it in a way that sounds fault-finding and superior, we may do more harm than good; but a word of warning, spoken at the right time and in the right way, is something that every Christian must be ready to speak.

iv. Light has one other characteristic—it is *revealing*. Light shows things up. We can see the faults in something, if it is put under a strong light.

It is here that there comes the hardest and the greatest Christian duty. It is the duty of living so finely that it shows up the life of the person who is not a Christian and makes him want to be a Christian. Negley Farson, the writer, once said of his grandfather whom he admired very much, 'I only know that he made other men look like mongrel dogs.' We have all met people who show others up, not deliberately, but without saying anything and just by being themselves.

At the end of this section comes a saying of Jesus which should keep us from all conceit and pride. We have been saying that we have got to be lights, that we have got to be seen, that we have got to be an example, that we have got to give a warning, that we have to live so finely that it shows others up. If we left it at that, it might well sound as if we were being told to say, 'Look at me! Look how good I am!' It might seem that we were trying to focus attention on ourselves. But see what Jesus says, 'Let your light so shine before men that they may see your good works, *and give glory to your Father who is in heaven.*' All this is not to get us glory, but to get God glory. How?

The way it ought to work is this. There ought to be something special in the life of the Christian, a courage and a kindness and an honesty and a purity that others do not have. This should make others ask, 'How does that person manage to live like that? How is his life so different from mine?' And the answer is, 'Because the person who lives like that has Jesus for his Friend and Helper'. Then the others may say, 'If Jesus can do that for him, I want Jesus as my friend, too.' To live finely is not to get credit for ourselves; it is to point others to the One who can make us live like that. A real

Christian life is worth a bushel of sermons when it comes to persuading people to become followers of Jesus.

We have to be the lights of the world. We must never be ashamed to show that we belong to Jesus. We must be an example to all. Sometimes we must speak a word of warning. Our life must show how a Christian can live and so make others want to share the Master who makes us able to live like that.

For Discussion

In what way can a Christian be an example to others?

CHAPTER FIFTEEN

Love and Law

Matthew 5:17-20

This is a very important section of the Sermon on the
Mount, which, if we study it and understand it, will save
us from making a mistake that we could quite easily make. It
tells us that to the end of the day a Christian must obey the
Law. To put this in the context in which we are thinking,
it means that, even after Jesus has come and has given us the
new law, the old law, the Ten Commandments with all their
sternness, still stands.

There is a certain danger in the Christian teaching. We
say that Jesus teaches us that God is love, and that we do not
need to be afraid of God any more. We say that Jesus teaches
us that God is our Father, and that he is willing and ready
to forgive us, whenever we ask him to do so. It would be easy
to go on from there and to say, 'Well, then, why shouldn't
I do what I like? If God loves me, he will forgive me anyway.
It will be all right in the end.'

Heine the great German philosopher was dying. He had
not been a Christian and he had not bothered much how he
lived, but he was not in the least worried. Someone asked
him why he was taking it all so calmly. 'God will forgive,'
he said, 'it is his trade.' The idea was that it made no
difference what we do; in the end God will forgive and there
will be no trouble and it will be quite all right.

This passage corrects this point of view, and tells us
that, even if God is love, and even if God forgives, that
does not mean that there are no laws and obligations any

more. We have only to think about this to see how true
it is.

i. If we really love someone, we do not allow him to do
exactly as he likes. Parents who really love their children do
not allow them to do exactly as they like. Teachers who are
really interested in their pupils do not let them behave
exactly as they like.

When children are very young, they often want to play
with dangerous things, like matches and fire and knives,
things that would injure and hurt them, if they were allowed
to do whatever they liked.

If we love a person, we discipline him; we control him;
we sometimes have to compel him to do what he ought to
do, and sometimes we have even to punish him when he will
not do it. It is easy to see that to let a person do exactly as
he likes might well be the worst possible thing for him; and
to let him do as he likes would be, not to love him, but to
spoil him.

God loves us, and for that very reason God has laid down
the right rules for life, and we suffer for it, if we break them.

ii. In the same way, if we are loved by someone, we should
not use that as a reason for doing what we like. If a young
person is loved by his parents, he should not say, 'I'll do
what I like. No matter what I do, they won't throw me out.
Whatever I do, they will still look after me.' He ought to say,
'I love my parents and they love me; and I must do my very
best not to hurt them or disappoint them or cause them
anxiety.'

The fact that he loves them and that they love him is the
very fact that keeps him from doing the wrong thing and
makes him do the right thing. It could happen that the young
person would not care much if he got into trouble for doing
something wrong. What stops him doing it is that he could

not bear to go home and meet his parents after he had done it. Love is not a reason for doing what we like; it is a reason for doing nothing to grieve those who love us.

iii. But why should the goodness that comes from love be greater and better and at the same time more difficult than the goodness which comes from Law? The Scribes and the Pharisees were the people who made Law the master of their lives, and our goodness has to exceed theirs. How can that be?

Think of it this way. If we are obeying the law, there is a definite limit to what we have to do. Suppose we buy something in a shop; we owe the shopkeeper the cost of the article. When we have paid the cost, we do not owe him any more. He has no further claim on us at all. But could we ever repay what we owe to our parents? We can by a payment satisfy a legal obligation; nothing we can do can ever pay for being loved.

Take another example. Suppose a young person did something which broke the law. He would be arrested; he would be tried; he would be sentenced. He might be put on probation; he might be fined; he might be sent to prison. But once he had completed the probation period, or paid the fine or served the sentence, he would be finished with the law; he would have completely satisfied its demands, and he could forget it. But he could never pay for the sorrow and the grief and the broken hearts he caused his parents by getting into trouble like that. You can always satisfy the claims of the law; if you give everything you have, you have not paid for being loved or for hurting love.

Now take this in regard to God. God loves us. So when we do a wrong thing, we do not only break God's law, we also break God's heart. And that is why sin is such a terrible thing.

iv. And so this section says one last thing to us. It says:

'Don't think it is easy to be a Christian'. Nothing worth while is ever easy. The way to the stars is always steep. The Greek poet Hesiod said, 'The gods have ordained sweat as the price of all things.' To be a Christian is going to take all we have got and more, because to be a Christian involves trying to show you are trying to deserve the love which has been shown to you by your loved ones and by God.

For Discussion

How can we demonstrate our love to God and to our fellow men?

CHAPTER SIXTEEN

Actions and Thoughts

Matthew 5:21-32

This is the most important section in the Sermon on the Mount, because in it we find the essential difference between the teaching of Jesus and the teaching of the Ten Commandments.

The difference is this. The Ten Commandments forbid murder; but the Sermon on the Mount goes further and forbids anger. It says in effect that to be angry with a man is just as bad as to murder him. The Ten Commandments forbid adultery; but the Sermon on the Mount goes further and forbids even the desire to commit adultery. It says in effect that to have this kind of desire is as bad as the thing itself.

This difference is very important. The Ten Commandments are concerned only with a man's outward actions; the Sermon on the Mount is concerned with his inmost feelings and desires. The Ten Commandments would be satisfied if a man abstained from murder, however much he wanted to kill someone else; and if a man abstained from adultery, however much he wanted to commit adultery. The Sermon on the Mount lays it down that what we want to do is quite as important as what we do, even if we do not do it.

Obviously, the standard of the Sermon on the Mount is very much higher than the standard of the Ten Commandments. A man can usually manage to control his actions, but it is a very different thing to control his thoughts and wishes and desires.

i. Quite clearly, Jesus was right. If we think that outward deeds are a test of goodness, we are never really safe, for we are completely dependent on self-control. We want to do the thing, but we do not do it. A situation like this means that there is always tension. It is like sitting on a volcano—we never know when the volcano will erupt. We never know when the self-control will snap. It is like having a tiger on a leash. So long as the leash holds, it is all right. But what happens if the leash breaks?

Plato described life as a situation in which the soul or what we would call the self is like a charioteer driving a chariot with two horses yoked to it. The one horse is gentle and biddable and well trained. That horse is *reason*. The other horse is wild and unmanageable and undisciplined. The name of that horse is *passion*. So Plato sees life as a continual struggle between reason and passion. To put the matter in biblical terms, so long as we can control ourselves with reason and discipline we can obey the Ten Commandments; but when passion gets a grip of us, we break them.

So long as we desire to do the wrong thing, we may possibly do it; and if the desire becomes strong enough, we will do it. And so Jesus was right to say that thoughts and feelings are every bit as important as deeds and actions, and that the only way to be really safe and really good is not only to do the right things, but not even to want to do the wrong thing.

ii. One interesting conclusion emerges from this. If this is so, only God and a man's own conscience know what kind of a man he is. A man may seem to be good; outwardly he may never do a wrong thing; he may even do fine things. But all the time he may be a walking civil war; he may all the time be wanting to do the wrong thing and struggling against it.

The Jews said that every man has two natures, the good and the bad, and that there is a constant struggle between the two. Sometimes they said that every man has two angels, a good angel trying to pull him up, and a bad angel trying to drag him down, and all life is a contest between the two.

We all know that this is true. We all know this struggle and this tension.

So it can happen that a man may present one appearance to the world and quite another appearance inside himself. God not only sees our deeds but also knows our thoughts (Psalm 139:2). Only God therefore really knows what kind of person we are. We can put on a show to others; we cannot put on a show to him.

iii. How can we ever satisfy this commandment of Jesus? How can we become such that we not only refrain from doing the wrong thing but do not even want to do it?

There is only one way to get rid of a wrong thought or desire. And that is not to say, 'I will not think of this. I must not want this.' When we try it that way, we only fix our thoughts more firmly on the wrong thing and on the forbidden desire. The only way to drive out one thought is to think some other thought; and the only way to drive out one desire is to get a still stronger desire.

We can take an example. A boy may want to laze about, to eat and drink too much, to smoke and generally to have a good time; but he may come to want to be a first-class athlete or a first-class football player. And if this second desire is strong enough, it will drive out the first, and the boy will forget all the things he used to want to do in the desire to become as fit as possible. The good desire has driven out the bad.

We can never in this life completely eliminate our wrong desires. Even Paul (Romans 7) had to say that there were still times when he found himself doing the things that he knew were wrong, and unable to do the things that he knew were right, because of this inner struggle and tension. But the more we know Jesus and the more we love him, the more we will want only to please him and only to be true to him; and the more we are committed to him, the less the lower things will appeal to us.

For Discussion

What is the value of worship in our attempts to control our thoughts?

CHAPTER SEVENTEEN

A Pledged Word

Matthew 5:33-37

When people make a solemn undertaking or make a solemn statement they often do so, as we say, on oath. They swear that they are telling the truth. A man may make a promise 'in the name of God' or, 'as I shall answer for it to God' or, 'before God'. In the law courts a man will swear by God to tell the truth, the whole truth, and nothing but the truth. In the marriage ceremony a couple will promise as they will answer for it to God to be loving and true to one another. An oath is always held to be a guarantee that a man is telling the truth, or that he will keep his promise.

The Jews are characteristically an honest people. They have a great respect and reverence for oaths. But in the time of Jesus some of them were masters of evasion. Their particular form of evasion was this. If in any promise or statement they actually introduced the name of God, then they would certainly speak the truth and certainly keep the promise, for they believed that in that case God had become, as it were, an actual partner in the transaction. But if they did not introduce the name of God, they felt quite free to evade the truth and not to keep their promise. So, if a Jew swore 'by God' or, 'in the name of God' or, 'as he would answer for it to God', his word could be taken absolutely. But if he swore 'by heaven' or, 'by the earth' or, 'by his own head', then he would not necessarily tell the truth, and he would not necessarily keep his promise. So the Jew had a kind of system of more or less binding oaths.

It was Jesus' teaching that it should not be necessary to use oaths at all, and that a simple 'yes' or 'no' should be quite enough to guarantee a statement or a promise.

Some people have taken this section as a total prohibition of all oaths in making statements or promises. For instance, the Quakers in a court of law refuse to take the oath; they will affirm that they will speak the truth, but they refuse to swear by God that they will do so. But this is not the real significance of this section. Jesus himself did not protest about being put upon oath. At his trial the High Priest said to Jesus, 'I adjure you by the living God, tell us if you are the Christ, the Son of God' (Matthew 26:63). That is, the High Priest demanded that Jesus should answer on oath; and Jesus did. When Paul was writing to the Galatians, and when he wanted to stress the fact that his account of events was accurate, he said: 'Before God, I do not lie' (Galatians 1:20). He put himself on oath. This does not rule out making statements and promises under oath. What it does is this.

i. It says in effect that it is all wrong to think of bringing God into any transaction; it is impossible to keep God out, because God is always present. Whether a promise is taken using the name of God or not, God is there and hears that promise. We do not make God a partner in a transaction only when we use his name; God, just because he is God, and just because he is present everywhere, is a witness to every statement and a witness to every promise.

This is simply a way of saying that we cannot say or promise anything anywhere without God hearing what we say. We must always remember that God is the unseen hearer of everything we say, and that therefore every word is spoken to God, and every promise is made to God. We cannot bring God in and put God out just as we wish; we cannot keep him out, however much we would wish to do so. A real Christian remembers that every time he speaks, he speaks to God.

ii. But this section says something else. Jesus ends by saying, 'Let what you say be simply Yes or No; anything more than this comes from evil.' What the last phrase means is this. The fact that we have to put people on oath at all results from an evil situation. It ought to be possible to accept a man's word without making him swear that he is telling the truth. It is only in a society in which we suspect men of lying that oaths become necessary.

The meaning for us is that we should show ourselves so absolutely trustworthy that everyone will know that when we speak, we speak the truth.

What this world needs more than anything else is people who can be trusted to speak the truth and to keep their promises, without the necessity of any oaths, and we must be like that.

For Discussion

Is it ever right to tell a lie?

CHAPTER EIGHTEEN

No Revenge

Matthew 5:38-42

Jesus begins by saying that under the old law, when any injury was done, it was quite right to insist on an eye for an eye, and a tooth for a tooth. This was indeed the principle of the Old Testament law (Exodus 21:24; Leviticus 24:20; Deuteronomy 19.21).

This old law is often quoted as an example of the savage and bloodthirsty laws of the Old Testament, but it is very far from being that; it is rather the first step towards mercy. In the ancient world, before the law of an eye for an eye and a tooth for a tooth was laid down, if any man did another man an injury, it was the duty of the whole tribe of the first man to do every possible injury to the whole tribe of the other man. And the revenge that was sought was not just the hurt of the men of the tribe who had done the wrong, but their death. This was what was known as the blood feud or the vendetta. The minute a wrong was done two whole tribes were at each other's throats trying to slaughter each other.

This law about the eye for the eye and the tooth for the tooth *limits vengeance*. It lays it down that, if a wrong is done, revenge can be taken only on the man who actually did the injury, and the revenge must be exactly the same as the harm he did, no more and no less. This put an end to the vendetta and the blood feud, and limited vengeance to the exact equivalent of the wrong that had been done.

This was a step in the right direction, and a step towards mercy, but, as Jesus saw it, it did not go nearly far enough.

Jesus laid it down that *there should be no revenge at all*. Then he went on to take three examples of the kind of thing he meant.

i. *If anyone strikes you on the right cheek, turn to him the other also.*

This is a more far-reaching saying than would appear at first sight. If a right-handed person is going to hit the right cheek of a person facing him, how must he do it? He cannot do it with the open palm of his right hand, as you would normally slap a person's face, unless he twists his hand round into such a position that he can get no force into the blow at all. Try it and see! The only way that a right-handed person can slap the right cheek of a person facing him is with *the back of his hand*. To flick a man with the back of the hand is a contemptuous thing to do; it is worse than a good slap in the face. And the Jewish law laid it down that a blow with the back of the hand is a double insult liable to double damages.

We now see what this saying of Jesus really means. It has really nothing to do with slapping people in the face. After all, if Christianity consisted in literally turning the other cheek when someone hit us, we would not get much chance to practise it, for people do not usually go about slapping each other's faces. What it does mean is: You must never resent and try to take revenge even for the most hurting insult that can be paid to you.

ii. *If anyone would sue you and take your coat, let him have your cloak as well.*

This again is much more far-reaching than at first sight it seems to be. A Jew wore two main articles of clothing. He wore an inner garment, like a shirt, called the *chitōn*, and here the *coat* is the *chitōn*. If a man got into debt and would not pay, it was quite legal for the creditor to take the man's *chitōn* from him. But the Jew also wore an outer robe, like a blanket, seven feet broad by three feet deep. He did not only wear this by day, he also slept in it at night; and this robe was regarded as essential, and so could not be taken even for debt (Deuteronomy 24:12, 13). This was the *himation*, the *cloak*. So Jesus says: If a man sues you, for your coat, your *chitōn*, which he can quite legally take from you, give him your cloak, your *himation* too, even though he has no legal right whatever to take it from you.

This means that a Christian must never insist upon his rights. There are many people who are always talking about their rights and insisting on getting them. The Christian is to be much more concerned about his responsibilities.

iii. *If anyone forces you to go one mile, go with him two miles.*

In the time of Jesus Palestine was an occupied country, under the dominion of the Romans. There was one specially humiliating law. A Roman soldier could compel any Jew to carry his baggage for one mile. When a Roman soldier wanted a Jew to do this, he would come up and tap him on the shoulder with the flat of his spear. That was a sign that the Jew, whether he liked it or not, had to carry the Roman's baggage for one mile. Jesus said: If that happens to you, go two miles.

What Jesus meant was this. It is never enough for a Christian to do just his duty; the Christian must always be ready to go beyond his duty, and to do far more than he can be compelled to do.

We all know the kind of person who does only the irreducible minimum, who does only what he has to do and not one stroke more, and who is very annoyed if he is asked to do anything extra. The Christian is the person who does his duty, and then willingly and voluntarily goes out of his way to do far more.

This passage tells us that the Christian must never resent an injury and must never try to retaliate for it; the Christian must never stand upon his rights; the Christian must never be content to do only his duty, but must always be ready and willing to do far more.

For Discussion

What is the point of doing these extra things?

CHAPTER NINETEEN

The Meaning of Christian Love

Matthew 5:43-48

There is more of the essence of the Christian life in this section than in any other passage in the Bible. Nothing is more characteristically Christian than the command of Jesus, 'Love your enemies', and this is the section which tells us most about Christian love.

Clearly, we have first of all to find out just what Christian love is. In English we have only one word for *love*, and it has to do duty for more than one kind of attitude and feeling. Greek is in many ways a far richer language than English and it has four words for love.

i. There is the word *erōs*. (The *o* is pronounced like the *ow* in the word *show*.) This is the word for the love of a man for a woman and it has always passion and sex in it.

ii. There is the word *storge*. (The final *e* is pronounced as the English *ae*.) This is the word for the love which exists between members of the same family, the love of son or daughter for father or mother, the love for kinsfolk and relations.

iii. There is *philia*. This is the word for warm affection. It has in it both spiritual and physical love; it would express the relationship which in English we describe by saying that two people love each other and would be used for the love between husband and wife.

iv. In this passage none of these words is used. The word used here is *agapē* (the final *e* is pronounced *ae*). This word does not occur in Greek at all outside the New Testament, although its corresponding verb does. As a noun it is a new word to describe a new attitude to people. Christianity demanded something new, and it had to find a new word to describe it.

What then does *agapē* mean? This section tells us. It is the kind of love that God has for men. And what is that? It is the love which makes the sun rise on the evil and on the good, and sends rain on the just and on the unjust. (In Palestine rain was not something to be disliked; in a dry country it was a blessed gift from God, which made the harvest grow, and for which men were devoutly grateful.) This, then, means that, whether a man is good or bad, God never fails to give him his good gifts. And this is to say, that whether a man is good or bad, God never ceases to treat him with kindness and with love.

Here we have the meaning of *agapē*, Christian love. Christian love is undefeatable goodwill, indestructible kindness, benevolence that cannot be stopped by anything the other person does. Christian love means that, no matter what anyone does to us, we will never allow ourselves to hate him or be bitter to him, but will always seek nothing but his highest good. However cruel he is to us, we will never be anything but kind to him. However he feels to us, we will feel nothing but goodwill to him.

It is quite clear that this kind of love is not the same as we have for our nearest and dearest. The great difference is that we love our nearest and dearest because we cannot help doing so. We speak of falling in love; this kind of love is something which happens to us with no effort on our part. But the other kind of love, the love of our enemies, is something which requires a conscious effort. We may put it this way. The love we have for our nearest and dearest is a thing of the heart; the love we have for our enemies is a thing of the will. It is not something which just happens; it is a victory.

Christian love will never allow itself to hate any man, and has won the power to love even the unlovely and the unlovable. No matter how it is treated, it has nothing but goodwill. And this kind of love is not a thing that comes easily and naturally; it can only come as a victory and a conquest of self. How is this victory to be won?

First, we have the example of Jesus. No matter what men did to him, Jesus would not stop loving them. They could insult him, they could deliberately misunderstand him, they could be disloyal to him, they could betray him, they could crucify him, and even then he prayed, 'Father, forgive them, for they know not what they do' (Luke 23:34). He is the great example of one who would never hate.

Second, we have the help of Jesus. If we try to be like him, he will certainly help us to be like him, and to have the same attitude to other people as he had.

There is just one other thing to be said. To have this undefeatable love for people is far away from letting them do anything and from letting them get away with anything. It could be the worst thing possible for a man never to be disciplined, never to be controlled, never to be made to realize that wrong-doing has its necessary consequences. This love is not an easy, soft, sentimental thing; it is a strong love, which knows that a man has often to be punished for his own good.

We must always remember that Christian love seeks, not to allow a man to do as he likes, but always his highest good, and his highest good may well involve his punishment.

For Discussion

How can Christian love best be shown? What is the connection between love and discipline?

CHAPTER TWENTY

The Peril of Self-Display

Matthew 6:1-6; 16-18

In this passage Jesus shows how even the best things can
go wrong, and even the most beautiful things become ugly,
if they are not done in the right way. To the Jew there were
three actions which were of the very essence of religion.

i. There was *almsgiving*, that is, the giving of gifts to those
who need them.

The Jews were always specially mindful of the poor. There
is a wonderful regulation in Deuteronomy 24:19-22. It is there
laid down that, if a man is reaping his field, or gleaning his
grapes, or gathering his olives, he should never collect the
last possible sheaf of grain and the last possible bunch of
grapes and the last possible cluster of olives; he should always
leave something for the poor people to come and gather for
themselves. This is to say that a man should always be ready
to share something of his harvest with people who have no
harvest of their own. In Proverbs 19:17 the Wise Man says,
'He who is kind to the poor lends to the Lord.'

To this day as a people the Jews always remember their
duty to their poorer fellow-Jews. To them giving is the act
of a good man, and something which pleases God.

ii. There was *prayer*. Prayer is a mainstay of any religion,
but it was specially so to the Jews. Every devout Jew prayed
three times a day, at 9 o'clock in the morning, at 12 midday,
and at 3 o'clock in the afternoon. They had a saying that a
man who prays in his home surrounds it with a wall of iron.

The Jew never failed to bring his thanks to God, to ask

God for forgiveness, to plead for God's help and guidance for life, and to commend his dear ones to the love and the care of God. To the Jew prayer was the mainspring of the good life.

iii. There was *fasting*. The devout Jew always fasted on Mondays and Thursdays, and every Jew fasted when he asked for forgiveness for some sin, or when he mourned the death of a loved one.

To a Jew fasting was two things. It was a way of showing God that he was really sorry. It was as if he said, 'Words are not enough to show God that I am sorry for the wrong things I have done; I will prove my sorrow by going hungry and thirsty for a time.' Second, fasting was self-discipline. The Jew gave up a pleasure for a time in order to show that it had not mastered him, but that he was master of it. The Jew did not fast just for fasting's sake, for the Jew had a saying that a man will give account to God for every good thing he might have enjoyed and did not enjoy. But the Jew also very wisely felt that, if you give up a thing for a time, you will enjoy it all the more when you come back to it.

Fasting was to the Jew a valuable discipline for life.

Almsgiving, prayer, and fasting were all great and valuable things; and yet Jesus points out that they could all go wrong. And they go wrong when a man does them for self-display.

i. A man spoils any gift when, as he gives it, he seems to say, 'Look how generous I am!' Some people are prepared to be generous only when everyone knows about it. If they give anything, they want to get the credit for it; they want everyone to know, and are not happy unless they are publicly thanked and praised. It is obvious that such people are not really concerned to help a poor man, but rather to win honour for themselves. It is not the needy person of whom they are thinking; they are thinking only of themselves.

At their best the Jews were not like that. Some of their

wisest teachers said that the best kind of giving is when a man does not know to whom he is giving and when the man who receives the gift does not know the donor.

We have to be careful about this. It is natural to want credit for what we do. But the real Christian never thinks of himself when he gives, but only of the person to whom he is giving.

ii. A man spoils prayer, when he prays in such a way as in effect to say, 'Look how religious I am.' He wants everyone to see how pious he is.

There were two ways in which the Jew could specially do this. As we have seen, the Jew prayed at 9 in the morning, at midday, and at 3 in the afternoon. When the hour came, one of these ostentatiously pious Jews would plump down in the middle of the pavement and say his prayers, and the more people there were to look on, the better he was pleased. It was customary to pray when entering the synagogue, and synagogues were often built at the corner of the street. So one of these ostentatiously pious Jews would stand at the door of the synagogue or on the steps leading up to it praying for a long time, in the hope that people would look at him and say what a very holy man he must be when he prays all that time.

Some people make a parade of their religion. The way in which they talk and dress and even walk is all designed to call attention to their special piety. Their one idea is to draw attention to themselves. They are not really thinking of God; they are thinking of themselves. They do not really pray to God; they pray to impress other people.

There is something wrong with man's religion when it becomes an act to make other people think how religious he is; we should be thinking always of God and of God alone when we pray or worship.

iii. A man spoils fasting, when he fasts in such a way that he is saying all the time, 'Look how earnest a Christian I am.'

A man may undertake some act of self-discipline and then talk about it and even boast about it all the time. He may talk about the things he has given up and about the habits he has mastered and about the time-table of discipline to which he lives, until it becomes quite clear that his one idea is to make people see what a wonderful person he is.

Of course, we have to have self-discipline in life, but the minute we practise self-discipline in order to let everyone else see it and to tell everyone else about it, it has gone completely wrong.

In everyone there is some touch of pride and of self-conceit. Everyone, if he is telling the truth, will have to admit that he likes people to think well of him. We have to be careful that we do not do the right things from the wrong motives; and to do things for our own glory is one of the worst motives of all.

For Discussion

When good and kind things are done in order to gain praise and credit for them, do they lose all their value?

CHAPTER TWENTY-ONE

The Lord's Prayer

Matthew 6:7-15

This section is of special importance for in it we have the prayer that Jesus taught his disciples to pray. Because we pray it so often, it is easy to gabble through it without thinking of what we are saying, and we are now going to try to remind ourselves what it really means.

Before we look at each part of it, we must look at it as a whole. When we do that, one thing immediately strikes us. In the Lord's Prayer we give God his proper place, before we even begin to ask anything for ourselves. We ask that God's name should be held in reverence, that God's kingdom should come, that God's will should be done, and only then do we begin to ask for the things that we need.

It is only when God is given *his* rightful place that all other things take *their* rightful place. If you wish to draw a circle of the right size and in the right place, the first thing that you must settle is the centre of the circle; get the centre right, then the circumference will be right. So, then, if we want to get life right, we must get the centre right, and once God is put in the centre of life, the rest will be right.

The prayer begins, *Our Father*. When Jesus prayed, he called God *Abba* (Mark 14:36), and Paul said that it is possible for us to do the same (Romans 8:15; Galatians 4:6). The word *Abba* was the word by which a little Jewish boy or girl called his or her father. To this day you will hear Jewish boys and girls shouting *Abba* through the house when they want

their father. This is to say, if you found this word in any
ordinary book, or if you wanted to translate the way in
which it is still used today, the only possible translation
would be 'Daddy'. We cannot translate it that way, because
it would sound so strange. But the word tells us that, when
we are praying to God, we are not praying to someone
remote; we are praying to someone who is close to us and who
loves us very much. When we are praying to God we do not
need to feel strange at all; we can just talk to him.

But he is our Father *in heaven*. This is the other side of
it. Besides being the One who is close and familiar to us,
God is the One who also has might and majesty and power.
If God was only love, he might want to help us and yet
not be able to. But because God is love *and* might, he is
able to help as no one else can. His love is backed by his
power.

We then ask that God's *name should be hallowed*. The Greek
word for *to hallow* literally means *to regard as different*. This
means that we ought to think of God as different from
anyone else. To put that in another way, it means that we
ought to give God a unique place in our life. To put that in
still another way, this means that we should reverence God.
Now what is the best way to show that we really reverence a
person? The best way is to obey him, to do only what pleases
him, to make him the one who really controls our life. So
what this petition really means is: 'O God, help me to give
you a unique place in my life. Help me to reverence you.
And help me to show that I reverence you by always remem-
bering you and always obeying you'.

We then go on to pray: *Thy kingdom come, thy will be
done in earth as it is in heaven*. These two phrases mean exactly
the same thing. If we are to be citizens of any kingdom, we
must obey the laws of that kingdom; and if we are to be

citizens of the Kingdom of God, we must obey the will of God. To be a member of the Kingdom of God and to do the will of God are one and the same thing.

It would be true to say that a Christian is a man who never again does what he likes, and who always does what God likes. When Jesus came into Paul's life, Paul's first question was, 'What shall I do, Lord?' (Acts 22:10). In every act and decision in life, we have to ask, 'Lord, what do you want me to do?'

A great many people when they pray are really praying, 'O God your will be *changed*'. They are asking that this or that should not happen, or that they should not have to do this or that. If the Christian knows that a thing has to be done, no matter how difficult it may be, he says to God, 'Your will be done.'

If we want to be members of God's Kingdom we must obey God's will.

We then go on to pray: *Give us this day our daily bread.* There are two things to be noted here.

First, this literally means: Give me bread for the coming day. This means that we are not praying to God for the distant future but for the coming day. And this tells us that our job is to live one day at a time and not to worry about the future. If we deal well with each day as it comes, then all the days will be good.

Second, it is bread that we pray for. This is to say that we pray for the essentials of life, not the luxuries. We pray to God for the necessities of life, for we as Christians are not meant to live luxuriously but to live well.

We then pray: *Forgive us our debts as we have forgiven our debtors.* This is a petition which ought to make us think very seriously indeed, for it literally means that we are asking God to forgive us *in proportion as* we forgive others. And

D

this means that, if we refuse to forgive others, we are asking God *not* to forgive us.

This is a line of thought which runs through the New Testament. Jesus said that it is the merciful who will receive mercy (Matthew 5:7). Jesus told a story of a debtor who was forgiven a very great debt and who went out and dealt completely unforgivingly with a man who owed him a very small debt. His master promptly withdrew the forgiveness of the debt and had him thrown into prison until he should pay every penny. Because he would not forgive, he could not be forgiven; and, said Jesus, that is what is going to happen to everyone who refuses to forgive. 'So also my heavenly Father will do to everyone of you, if you do not forgive your brother from your heart' (Matthew 18:23-35). James said, 'Judgment is without mercy to one who has shown no mercy' (James 2:13).

We ought to think twice and more than twice before we dare to pray this petition. If we pray it after saying, 'I will never forgive so and so for what he did to me', then we are asking God not to forgive us. If we pray it while we have an unhealed quarrel with someone, then we are praying not to be forgiven. Once Robert Louis Stevenson abruptly stopped in the middle of the Lord's Prayer when he came to this petition. 'I am not fit to pray the Lord's Prayer today,' he said.

We must always remember that we cannot receive forgiveness, unless we give forgiveness.

The Lord's Prayer finishes: *Lead us not into temptation, but deliver us from evil.* It has always puzzled people why we should ever think that God should *tempt* us. We generally take the word *tempt* to mean *try to persuade a man to do the wrong thing*. In Genesis 22:1 (in the AV) we read, 'God did tempt Abraham'. Quite clearly, this cannot mean that God tried to make Abraham sin. What then does it mean? If we look at the RSV in Genesis 22:1 we find that it says, 'God tested Abraham'. Here is the solution.

What we are really praying is that God should not test us too severely. A boy in training might say to his trainer, 'Don't give me too big a test.' In this prayer we are saying to God, 'Please don't send too big a test to me in life, but, if such a test does come, then help me to come safely through it.'

Any test is meant to make a man stronger and fitter and more able to do the work God meant him to do. If we are tempted, and if we are given a big and difficult thing to do, we must say to ourselves, 'This is a test. Help me not to let myself down and not to let God down.'

The next time we pray the Lord's Prayer we must remember all these things. We must not just thoughtlessly repeat it, but must think of the meaning of each petition as we pray it.

For Discussion

Which petition of the Lord's Prayer is most real to us?

D*

CHAPTER TWENTY-TWO

The Things that Matter

Matthew 6:19-24

One of our instincts is that of acquisitiveness. Kept in its place this is obviously a good instinct, for it enables us to save and to plan, and to earn and to get the things we need to support our own life and the lives of those dependent on us. This is the instinct which enables a man to make a house and a home. But if this instinct gets out of control, it is equally obviously a bad thing, for it can turn a man into a miser, or into a man whose one aim in life is to get all he can and to keep everything to himself and for himself.

Clearly, one of the great secrets of the good life will be to want the right things. This is what this section is about.

Jesus says that we must want the things which last and which will never deteriorate. So he takes three examples of the things that no one should ever give his heart to, because they do not last, or because they can be very easily lost.

There are the things which *the moth can consume*. This means clothing. In the ancient world clothing was regarded as wealth. The AV speaks of *changes of raiment;* usually in these places the RSV speaks of *festal garments;* both words mean magnificent and costly clothes. So Joseph specially honours Benjamin by giving him five festal garments (Genesis 45:22); Samson offers thirty festal garments to anyone who can solve his riddle (Judges 14:12); Naaman brings with him ten festal garments for anyone who will cure his leprosy (2 Kings 5:5). So Jesus says, Some people spend their lives acquiring magnificent clothing. They reckon this as wealth.

But the best clothing in the world will wear out and in the store-house the moths will get it.

There are the things which *the rust will consume*. This means suits of armour. If ordinary clothing was valuable, elaborately made armour was far more valuable. But in the long run, even if it is made of the finest metal, the rust will eat into it. A possible alternative reading is, not things which the *rust* consumes, but things which the *worm* consumes. This would be stores of grain. The wealth of the farmer would be in his grain and in his granaries; but the worm can get into the grain and the whole store can go bad.

There are the things which *the thieves can steal*. The word for *break in* literally means *to dig through*. The walls of Palestinian houses were made of hardened earth or clay and the thief could literally dig through them and effect an entry. The things which the burglar can steal are all kinds of material possessions and money. It is not wise, Jesus says, to make them your aim, for the thief and the burglar may steal them at any time.

Jesus says that it is foolish to collect things which inevitably deteriorate and things which can very easily be lost. So he says that we must lay up treasure for ourselves *in heaven*. This means that the really valuable things are the things we can take with us when we die. Quite clearly, we cannot take any material things with us when we die. Job said that he came into the world naked and he would leave it naked (Job 1:21); Paul writes to Timothy: 'We brought nothing into the world, and we cannot take anything out of the world' (I Timothy 6:7). We certainly cannot take clothes and armour and crops and material things and money with us when we die. What can we take with us? What can we lay up in heaven?

The answer is clear. The only thing that we can take to

heaven is *ourselves*. To put that in another way, the only thing that we can take with us when we leave this world is the character we have acquired during our stay in it. Therefore, the most important thing to acquire in this life is a fine character. The second part of this section, verses 22-24, tells us of two main ingredients in this character.

i. Verses 22 and 23 tell us of a certain kind of eye which we must have. The AV calls it the *single* eye; the RSV and the NEB both call it *sound* eye. The Greek word is *haplous*, and it literally does mean *single*. But it had one special meaning, and this special meaning, which Moffatt uses in his translation, is most probably right. *Haplous* can mean *generous;* and what Jesus is insisting upon is the *generous* eye.

The first item in the good character is *generosity*. Paul remembered that Jesus had said, 'It is more blessed to give than to receive' (Acts 20:35), or, as the NEB translates it, 'Happiness lies more in giving than in receiving.' Jesus' parable (Matthew 25:31-46) tells us that we will be judged by what we gave. There is a saying which runs, 'What I kept, I lost; what I gave, I have.'

An old fable tells how two men went to heaven. The one had been rich but utterly selfish, never giving anything away, the other had been poor, but generous with everything he had. The two men were taken to the houses they were to occupy in heaven. The poor man who had been generous was taken to a magnificent house; the man who had been rich and selfish was taken to what was no more than a hut. He was offended at this, especially when he compared it with what the poor man had received. He complained bitterly about it, and the angel who had taken him to it said, 'Well, you see, this is all we could build for you with the materials you sent up.' This man had been so selfish on earth that he had no treasure in heaven. It is characteristic of God that God so loved the world that he *gave* (John 3:16), and the Christian must be like that. To be generous is to lay up treasure in heaven.

ii. The second item in the good character is *loyalty*. You can't serve two masters, Jesus said. You can't serve God and mammon. *Mammon* is a word which stands for all material things. The NEB has, 'You cannot serve God and Money.'

This means that we must give our first loyalty to Jesus. All our lives we must ask of any course of action, not, Is it profitable?, but, Is it right? We must ask, not, How much do I make out of this?, but, Is this what Jesus wants me to do?

This is what a true Christian does. Full members of the Church come to what we sometimes call the Sacrament of the Lord's Supper. This word *sacrament* means many things, but at the moment there is one that we ought to note. The Latin word *sacramentum* means a *soldier's oath of loyalty*. It was a pledge that a Roman soldier took when he joined the army that he would be forever true to his Emperor and to his general. The Christian is a man who has pledged his absolute loyalty to Jesus Christ. And the command and the promise are, 'Be faithful unto death, and I will give you the crown of life' (Revelation 2:10).

Generosity to men and loyalty to Jesus—these are the two things which will give us a character which will be treasure in heaven.

For Discussion

What else may we treasure on earth, that will be continued in heaven?

CHAPTER TWENTY-THREE

Don't Worry

Matthew 6:25-34

We must be sure that we know what Jesus is saying in this passage. The AV is misleading. The essence of the passage is in verse 34. There the AV has, 'Take no thought for the morrow.' That sounds as if we were never to think ahead, never to make any provision for the future, never to try to exercise a prudent foresight. Some people have argued that this is what the passage does mean, and they have even gone on to argue that it is wrong for a Christian to take out an insurance policy, because that is taking thought for the morrow. But this is not what the passage means. The Greek word which in the AV is translated *thought* means *anxious thought*. The newer translations put this right. Both the RSV and the NEB have, 'Do not be anxious about tomorrow,' and Moffatt has, 'Never be troubled about tomorrow.' The simplest and the best translation would be, 'Don't worry about tomorrow.'

Never to think about the future at all would not be the action of Christian faith; it would be the action of reckless irresponsibility. It would, for instance, be the action of dishonest irresponsibility to buy something without thinking whether or not we could pay for it. It would be reckless to start out on some enterprise without counting the cost. Jesus himself said that the man who begins to build a tower without being certain that he can pay for it, and the man who goes to war without reckoning up the strength of the opposition, are very foolish men (Luke 14:28-32). Jesus always insisted that anyone who proposed to follow him should know exactly what he was doing (cp. Luke 9:57-62). This is not a command or an excuse to plunge recklessly into things with never a thought for how they are to be worked out and completed. If a boy was trying to be an athlete, or to get into a football team, he would be very foolish if he never did any training or preparation, and if he never thought of the future at all. What Jesus forbids is not wise thought for the future but unwise worry about it. How then ought we to face the future?

i. We should do everything we possibly can, and then stop worrying.

If we are honest about it, we will probably have to admit that, when we do worry, a good deal of our worry is due to the fact that we know that we are not as well prepared as we ought to be. If we are worried about an examination, for instance, it is very likely because we know quite well that we have not done the work for it. Worry and lack of preparation go hand in hand. So the first rule is to do our very best, and then go on.

ii. There are in life two kinds of things; the things about which we can do something, and the things about which we can do nothing. There are certain things which have to be accepted, and it is never any good worrying about the things that cannot be changed. To do that is just as silly as to bang our heads against a brick wall. What cannot be cured has got to be endured.

iii. A good deal of worry would be avoided if we remembered that the real way to meet life is not to think in terms of escaping things, but to think in terms of facing and conquering them. Often people worry about how to avoid something that they see coming. There can be no peace of mind that way. But when we decide we have got to go on and face this, that very act of decision stops us worrying, for action is always one of the best cures for worry. If we say, not, How can I escape this?, but, How can I overcome this?, then a great many of our worries will come to an end, just because we have decided to face things and not go on running away from them.

iv. The longer we live the more we come to see that things are rarely so bad in actual fact as we expected them to be. The proverb says that it is no good crossing bridges until we come to them, and experience teaches us that the things we dread most are often not nearly as bad as we feared.

v. We ought always to remember that very often to worry about a thing is the best way to unfit ourselves to face it when it comes. Worry makes us less efficient. If we lose sleep worrying about an examination or about how we will play in a game, all it does is to make us less able to sit the examination and less likely to play well. Worry makes things worse instead of better.

vi. The New Testament tells us that, whatever happens to us, nothing can happen to us that we cannot bear. 'God,' says Paul, 'will not allow you to be tested above your powers' (I Corinthians 10:13 NEB). No matter what will come to us, we can face it.

vii. Last of all, we can be certain that, whatever we have to do or bear, we do not have to do and to bear it alone. Jesus promised to be with us always, and he will keep his promise.

For Discussion

What worries us most? Can anything be done about it?

CHAPTER TWENTY-FOUR

Warning to Critics

Matthew 7:1-5

This section has a warning for almost everyone. Almost everyone is a natural critic. If we see a group of people talking together, the chances are that they will be talking about someone else and criticising him.

In this matter of criticising others Jesus lays down a principle which is obviously true in this world, but which, he says, has also implications for eternity. Jesus' principle is: Don't criticise others if you don't want them to criticise you, because others will certainly treat you in the way in which you treat them. In life we get what we give, and if we give criticism, we will also receive criticism.

But Jesus would take this principle beyond this world. He had in fact already done so in what he said about forgiveness. He said that the man who wishes to obtain the forgiveness of God must himself first forgive his fellow men; and just so, if a man is a stern judge of his fellow men, he cannot expect God to be anything other than a stern judge to him. If we want to find God kind, we too must be kind. Others will treat us as we treat them, and God's judgment of us depends on how we have judged others.

There are certain clear reasons why we should not judge and criticise others. Some of them Jesus definitely lays down; others we can deduce from our knowledge of the way in which a Christian should live.

i. First and foremost, only the person who is himself perfect has the right to criticise other people, and there is no one who is perfect.

Jesus had a sense of humour, and sometimes said things that must have made his audience smile. He did so on this occasion. He said that when we criticise other people, it is like a man with a plank in his own eye trying to take a speck of dust out of another man's eye. Let the man remove the plank from his own eye, before he proceeds to try to remove specks of dust from someone else's eye.

There is an old saying which lays it down that 'there is so much bad in the best of us and so much good in the worst of us that it ill becomes any of us to criticise the rest of us'. We have quite enough faults of our own without criticising the faults of other people. So then the first law of criticism would be this—take a good look at yourself before you start looking critically at other people.

ii. Next, we have no right to criticise other people, unless we have gone through the same experiences as they. The Indians have a proverb: 'No man has a right to find fault with another man, until he has walked a mile in his moccasins'.

It is easy for a man with a placid, easy-going temperament to criticise a man with a hot temper. But instead of criticising him he should try to understand him. As one man with a quick temper said to another man who was finding fault with him, 'I have to control more temper in five minutes than you have to control in five years.' It is easy for a person who has no strong passions to criticise a man whose passions are violent. It is easy for a man who has lived a sheltered life to criticise a man who never really had a chance. When George Whitefield, the famous preacher, saw a man being taken out to be hung for a crime, he said, 'There but for the grace of God go I.' He meant that, if he had come from the same background and had the same upbringing as the other man, he too might well have been a criminal.

Before ever we criticise another it is always necessary that

we should try to understand him, and to understand why
he acted as he did. The French have a proverb: 'To know all
is to forgive all.' When we try to understand another's
experience we are more likely to sympathise than to criticise.

iii. No one has any right to criticise, unless he is prepared
at least to try to do better than the person he is criticising.
We all know the kind of people who are what we could call
arm-chair critics. They will never do anything themselves
but are quick to criticise everyone else. The person who
hurls abuse at players from the terracing would probably do
a lot worse himself if he was on the field. The person who
criticises the way some activity is run will often make no
attempt to do the running of it himself. There is a kind of
person—all too common—who refuses all work and dodges
all responsibility, and who yet continually criticises. Remember that if we claim the right to criticise we have to accept the
duty of trying to do better.

iv. There is a general rule of life which we cannot remember too often. The person who *encourages* is much more
valuable than the person who *discourages*. An ounce of praise
is worth a ton of criticism. There is a rule of the Royal Navy
which says: No officer shall speak discouragingly to any other
officer in the discharge of his duties. The critic is out to
discourage, and the people who discourage others are a bad
debt in any circle in which they move.

v. There is still another thing to remember. We must
always try to take a man as a whole. A man may make one
mistake, but we have got to set against his one mistake all
the good things he has done. A man may have a fault, but
we have to set against that fault all the good qualities he has.
It is only when we take the whole man into consideration
that we can judge him. A man might be irritable because he
is suffering pain that no one knows about, or because he is

worried about some problem that he cannot share with anyone.

This is exactly why the only person who can really judge anyone is God. Only God knows all about us and therefore only God can judge. The right thing to do is to leave all judgment to God.

For Discussion

Is there a place for criticism? When does it do good and when does it do harm?

CHAPTER TWENTY-FIVE

Those Who Cannot be Taught

Matthew 7:6

At first sight this seems a hard saying, but it is simply laying down a universal truth. It says that there are only certain people to whom you can teach certain things.

We actually work on this principle in all teaching. A boy has to pass an entrance examination before he can get into a college or a university. We clearly could not teach the binomial theorem to someone who had not even begun to learn algebra; someone who did not know a word of Latin could not start reading Cicero or Virgil. If someone was learning how to play the piano, he would not start with Bach's Preludes and Fugues. We have to possess a certain kind of equipment before we can begin on certain kinds of study.

In all study the basic equipment that we need is humility. A person has to admit his own ignorance before he can even begin to learn. A famous Roman teacher said of some of his pupils, 'They would doubtless have been excellent students if they had not been convinced of their own wisdom.' No one can teach anything to the man who thinks he knows it all already. But the more a man knows the more he realises there is to know, and there is no one so humble as the really wise man. Conceit is the biggest barrier to learning.

But there is another kind of learning, the learning that we have to do from Jesus. To learn from Him we need specially two things. We need *reverence*. We need to feel that in the presence of Jesus we are in the presence of someone who is more than a man. Charles Lamb was once in a group of people who were discussing what they would do if certain great figures in history entered the room. They talked of all kinds of people. When they had talked of everyone they could think of, Charles Lamb said quietly, 'If Shakespeare came into this room, we would all stand up to do him honour, but if Jesus Christ entered this room, we would all kneel down to kiss the hem of his garment.' Once Napoleon was in a group of people who thought that they were clever and who were belittling Jesus and saying that He was only a man. Napoleon had been very quiet and then suddenly he said, 'Gentlemen, I know men, and Jesus Christ was more than a man.' To learn from Jesus we need the reverence which will listen and accept what he says.

The second thing we need in order to learn from Jesus is *love*. If we read the stories of the Resurrection, we will find one very interesting and significant thing. Jesus only appeared to those who loved him. He did not appear to Annas or Caiaphas or Pilate, but to Mary Magdalene and to Peter and to the two on the road to Emmaus who were talking about him. We must love Jesus before we can really learn the things that he wishes to teach us.

There is a reverse side to this which is even more of a warning. If a man can fit himself to hear and learn certain things, equally he can unfit himself to do so. If a lad does not study as he ought, he unfits himself to go on to further studies. If a lad does not keep himself fit, he unfits himself for athletics and games. This is true of our minds, too. If we never read anything but trivial books, if we never see anything but cheap and trivial plays and films, then in the end we come to a stage where we are unable to do any serious reading and thinking at all.

It is a law of nature that, if we do not use a faculty, we

lose it. If we never moved an arm or leg, we would end up by being paralysed.

It is the same with the biggest things of life. If we never listen to the voice of conscience, in the end we silence it. If we refuse to listen to Jesus speaking to us, we end up by becoming deaf to his voice. Think of it this way. The first time we do a wrong thing, we do it with a feeling of fear and hesitation; if we do it twice, it is easier to do it the second time; and, if we go on doing it, the time will come when we can do it without a tremor or a thought. We must remember that we can unfit ourselves for the most important things in life, if we stifle the voice of conscience and refuse to listen to the warnings and the commands of Jesus.

We must always strive to make ourselves fit to be taught and to do the fine things, and we must always avoid anything which would make us unfit for them.

For Discussion

How can we learn from God?

CHAPTER TWENTY-SIX

Asking and Receiving

Matthew 7:7-11

This section has been rightly called The Charter of Prayer. In it Jesus tells us to ask God for his gifts and we will receive them; to seek for his help and we will find it; to knock at his door and we will never find it closed against us.

How can we be sure this is so? Jesus argues from earth to heaven. A human father would never give his son a stone if he asked for bread, or a poisonous serpent if he asked for a fish. Well, then, Jesus argues, if a human father for all his faults can be depended on to give his son good gifts, how much more can you depend on God, in his perfect love, to give us his good gifts? God, the great Father, can never be less loving than an earthly father, and, if a son can count on an earthly father for help, how much more we can count on God.

Does this mean we will get anything we ask for? Does this mean we have only to ask in order to get? We have only to read this carefully to see that Jesus never even suggested that. He did not say that God would give us *any* thing; he said that God would give us *good* things. So then, in the light of this there are certain things that we must remember when we pray.

i. We must remember that God will never give us anything that would harm us. A child will often want to play with things that might seriously injure him; things, for instance, like fire, or a sharp knife, and, of course, a wise parent will not allow him to do so. Often a child would like as a gift something that would really do him no good at all, something that he would quickly get tired of, something in the end that would become just trouble and a nuisance.

When we are young, and even when we are fully grown up, we often do not really know what is good for us, and we often want the wrong things. We must therefore always remember that sometimes, if God gave us what we wanted, it would do us nothing but harm. God knows much better than we do what is for our good, and therefore God must sometimes say No to our prayers.

There is a story about Vane and Hampden, two of the greatest of seventeenth century Englishmen, and two of the most famous champions of freedom. When things were at their worst in the early days of Charles the First's reign, they determined to emigrate to America. They hoped that there, in the new colony, they would find the freedom they desired. They were actually on board ship in the Thames ready to leave, when a message came from the king forbidding them to leave the country. They stepped ashore bitterly disappointed. But the fact that they were prevented from going to America brought it about that they became two of the greatest members of Parliament, two of the leaders of the struggle for freedom, two of Cromwell's right-hand men. Their disappointment led to far greater things.

Very often what we count as disappointments turn out to be blessings. This is God saying No to us and then giving us some bigger thing, and so answering our prayers, not in our way, but in his.

ii. There is a fact about prayer that perhaps we do not remember enough. God does not listen only to *our* prayers; he has to listen to the prayers of all men everywhere. It is easy to see how two different people could be praying for different and even opposite things. So the second rule is that God will never give us something which will hurt some-one else.

We might, for instance, want to get ahead of someone in business. We might pray for it. But God will never answer a prayer that is the prayer of self-ambition, and which is really a prayer that someone else should be hurt in order that we may be helped.

We could put it this way—God will never answer a selfish prayer. We are all in God's family, and there is no favouritism in the family of God.

iii. These things are important, but there is a third fact about prayer which is more important than any other. *God will never do for us what we can do for ourselves*. We have always to do our utmost to make our own prayers come true.

We pray in the Lord's Prayer: Give us this day our daily bread. But that does not mean we can then sit back and wait for a loaf baked and sliced and paid for to fall into our lap. It is God who gives us our daily bread, because it is God who makes every seed to grow, but we have to work to earn that bread and to produce it. It is not God doing it for us; it is we and God doing it together.

If we are ill, there is no point in asking God to make us well again, unless we carefully carry out the doctor's instructions. We have to do our part in making the prayer come true. There is no point in asking God to make us good and wise, unless we are prepared to fight against our temptations and to study as hard as we can. Before the Battle of Dunbar Cromwell issued a famous order to his soldiers: 'Trust in God and keep your powder dry'. There was no point in trusting, unless they, too, did everything they could.

There is no one kinder than God to the person who tries, even if he fails; but not even God can help the man who is too lazy to help himself.

Jesus tells us to ask and to seek and to knock. God will give us the good things we need, but we must remember that he knows best, that he will never give us what would hurt someone else, and that prayer does not mean God doing things for us, but God giving us the strength to do them for ourselves.

For Discussion

Is prayer always asking for things?

CHAPTER TWENTY-SEVEN

The Golden Rule

Matthew 7:12

'Whatever you wish that men would do to you, do so to them.'
This, Jesus said, is the summing up of all that practical
religion means.

Almost every other religion has a saying something *like*
this, but with a significant difference. To take one example,
the Jews tell of how a Gentile came to their great teacher
Hillel and said, 'I will become a convert to Judaism, if you
can tell me the whole of the law while I stand on one leg.'
Hillel at once said, 'Do not do to anyone else what you would
not like him to do to you—in that one sentence there is the
whole of religion.'

That saying of Hillel is very like the saying of Jesus, and
yet there is a world of difference. The saying of Hillel is
negative. All that it asks is that we should not do to others
what we would not like them to do to us; it asks us to refrain
from doing certain things. And it is in this negative form
that this saying appears in almost all, if not quite all, other
religions. The saying of Jesus is positive. It asks that we
should actually go out of our way to do to others what we
would like them to do to us. We cannot fulfil it by *not* doing
things; we can only fulfil it by actively doing things for others.

It is one thing to avoid doing a man a bad turn—that would
satisfy Hillel's rule; it is quite another thing to do him a good
turn—that is Jesus' rule. It is one thing not to cheat a man;
it is quite another thing to be generous to him. It is one
thing not to hit a man when he is down; it is quite another

thing to pick him up and set him on his feet and start him off again.

It can be seen at once that the saying of Jesus demands far more than the saying of Hillel does. It is not enough that we should abstain from hurting someone; as Jesus sees it, we should go out of our way to help others.

If we are going to fulfil this demand, there are three things that we will need.

i. We will need *the seeing eye*. We will need to see when a person is in need. Many people never even notice other people's troubles. In the parable which tells of God's last judgment Jesus' complaint against the people who were condemned was 'I was hungry and you gave me no food, I was thirsty and you gave me no drink, I was a stranger and you did not welcome me, naked and you did not clothe me, sick and in prison and you did not visit me.' And these people answered, 'Lord, when did we see thee hungry or thirsty or a stranger or naked or sick or in prison, and did not minister to thee?' (Matthew 25:42-44). They had seen all right, but they had never noticed. They were so busy looking at themselves that they never noticed anyone else.

This may still happen. A lad may live at home and never see the help that he could give in the house. He can mix with other people and never notice if someone is under the weather or in trouble. We may be quite blind to other people's troubles and needs.

The first thing we need if we are to obey this command is the ability and the willingness to see what needs to be done.

ii. We will need *the sympathetic heart*. It is quite possible to see and not to care. This is what happened to the rich man in the parable of the rich man and Lazarus (Luke 16:19-31). He was clothed in the most magnificent clothes and ate the most luxurious meals; Lazarus was sick and helpless and poor and starving. Every day in life the rich man saw Lazarus lying at his gate; and it never dawned on him that Lazarus had anything to do with him. That is exactly why he finished up in hell.

This is what brought condemnation on the priest and the Levite in the parable of the good Samaritan (Luke 10:29-37). They saw the wounded man, but did not think it had anything to do with them, and so hurried past.

Everyone can see poverty and slums and bad working conditions. What makes a great social reformer is that he not only sees these things, he also feels them. They go through his eyes into his heart.

No Christian should ever look at someone in any kind of trouble without feeling compassion in his heart. There is no more unchristian thing than to see a person in trouble, even if it is his own fault, and to feel no sympathy for him.

iii. But we need a third thing to obey Jesus' command. We need the seeing eye, the sympathetic heart, and we need *the helping hand*. It is easy to see someone's trouble, to feel sorry for him, and still to do nothing about it. James condemns people like that. He writes, 'If a brother or sister is ill-clad and in lack of daily food, and one of you says to them, "Go in peace, be warmed and filled," without giving them the things needed for the body, what does it profit?' (James 2:15, 16). There is not much use seeing and sympathising without doing anything about it.

In regard to this there is one thing specially to remember. If we feel that we would like to help someone or some good cause, we should act on the generous impulse *at once*, for, if we put it off, we are not likely to do anything at all. The psychologist tells us that the oftener we put off acting on some fine feeling and the longer we put off a decision, the less likely we are ever to act or ever to decide. If we feel a desire to help, we should help at once.

We have not only not to do to others what we would not want them to do to us; we have to go out of our way actively to do to them what we would like them to do to us, and for that we need the seeing eye, the sympathetic heart, and the helping hand.

For Discussion

How would we like other people to treat us?

CHAPTER TWENTY-EIGHT

The Hard Way

Matthew 7:13, 14

In this section Jesus is laying down a universal law of life, and the law is that nothing worth getting can be got easily. The road to the greatest things is always steep and hard. The Greek poet Hesiod said, 'The gods have ordained sweat as the price of all things.' The famous Latin proverb has it: *Per ardua ad astra*, the way to the stars is steep.

It is this way in study. No one can get a good degree, and no one can get a good job or carve out a good career without hard work. The jobs which are got easily are almost always dead-end jobs. It is this way in athletics. No boy can ever become a first-class athlete or a first-class player of any game without working at it and without the strictest training. It is this way with any accomplishment. We can never become first-class at anything without work. There are certain things that money can buy, but the only coin that will buy real achievement is work. If this is so, it means that we must acquire certain qualities.

i. We must have *discipline*. Discipline means training, and it means training accepted, not in spasms, but constantly and unremittingly. It means the ability and the determination to go on with the training, even when we would very much like to be doing something else. It means not letting anything interfere with the programme which we have set ourselves, or which our trainers have mapped out for us.

Paderewski was one of the greatest pianists in the world. He practised for no less than eight hours each day. And he used to say, 'If I stop practising for one day, I know it; if I stop for two days, those who know me best can tell; if I stop for three days, my audiences can tell.' He could only reach and keep up his standards by unremitting toil.

ii. We must have a *goal*. We will accept anything in the way of work and discipline, if we think that in the end it is going to be worth while. We can accept the hardness of the road, if at the end there is something really great.

Nowadays things are much easier for students with government grants to help to support them, but a hundred years ago things were very different. Sir James Barrie tells of three students who shared a room with two camp beds and who had only one set of books between them. Two slept while the third studied, and then they changed places which often meant that one of them had to work all night to get his chance of the books and the bed. To this day there are in Glasgow in the first two university terms holidays which come exactly half-way through the term. These are still called Meal Mondays. A hundred years ago they were the days when students went back home for a fresh barrel of meal, for they existed mainly on porridge. The students of those days were willing to accept this because they saw at the end of it a degree which would make them a doctor, or a teacher, or a lawyer, or a minister. They believed that the greatness of the goal made the hardness of the way worth while.

And, of course, the Christian has a goal, not only in this life, but after this life, not only on earth but in heaven. The writer of the Letter to the Hebrews said that Jesus endured the cross and despised the shame *for the joy that was set before him* (Hebrews 12:2). Jesus was able to go through all his pain and humiliation for the sake of the glory that lay beyond for him in heaven. Even if the Christian life is hard, the reward is great. And if we set our eyes on it, we will know that everything is worth while.

iii. There is a simple way to put all this. It is to say that the greatest virtue in life is *perseverance*. Perseverance is not a romantic virtue. It means the ability to keep on going when the rest have stopped. Life is not a sprint; it is a marathon race; and in a marathon race it is the man who sticks it out to the end who gets there and wins the prize.

The trouble about so many people is that they are good at starting things but not at finishing them. We start collecting this or that; we start learning this or that; but we get tired of it; and it is thrown aside so that life is littered with things we began and never finished. Jesus said, 'He who endures to the end will be saved' (Matthew 10:22; 24:13).

The way to the best things is hard, but, given discipline and a goal and perseverance, we can get there.

For Discussion

What are we working for?

CHAPTER TWENTY-NINE

The Only Test

Matthew 7:15-23

The central thought of this passage is quite clear. You can judge a tree only by its fruits, and you can judge a man only by his deeds. The real test of a man is not what he *says*, but what he *does*. Robert Louis Stevenson once said of a man, 'I cannot hear what you say for listening to what you are.' Jesus said, 'There is no point in calling me Lord, if you do not accept my will for your life.'

There are two kinds of faith. There is that which is intellectual belief. This is the faith which accepts things with the mind. It may come in either of two ways. It may come because I accept the word of someone whom I believe to have the knowledge which gives him the right to speak. I believe that light travels at the speed of 186,000 miles per second, not because I can see it or prove it, but because the scientists tell me so, and I believe that they have the right to speak. This is intellectual faith on the basis of authority. Second, this faith may come because by the exercise of my mind I can prove something. I believe that the square on the hypotenuse of a right-angled triangle equals the sum of the squares on the other two sides, because Pythagoras proved it, and with my mind I can follow his proof.

This purely intellectual faith does not necessarily affect my conduct. My belief about the speed of light and my belief about right-angled triangles do not make any difference to what I do every day. They are things which I accept with my mind, but do not translate into everyday action.

The other kind of faith is much more than mental accept-
ance of something as true; it is a faith which affects my
conduct all the time. Since I believe that ten and ten make
twenty, no one is going to make me pay 25p for two 10p
articles. This is something which I not only mentally and
intellectually accept; it is something on which I *act*.

Christian faith is this second kind of faith. Christian faith
has to be worked out in deeds. 'Faith,' said James, 'apart
from works is dead' (James 2:26). Christian faith must be not
only something which we accept with our minds, but
something which we live with our whole lives. A man's
Christian faith ought to determine the kind of person he is.
This is just what Jesus is saying—a man's faith is known by
his life. If this is so, what kind of life proves that a man is a
Christian? With what kind of action must he back up his
words?

A sentence in John's first Letter (I John 3:10) gives us the
answer very shortly, 'By this it may be seen who are the
children of God, and who are the children of the devil:
whoever does not do right is not of God, nor he who does
not love his brother.' Here are the two tests of the Christian
—personal purity and love for others. Let us look at them.

i. First, there is the test of *personal purity*. John says,
'If we say we have fellowship with him while we walk in
darkness, we lie' (I John 1:6). That is, if we claim to be
the friends of Jesus and do all the wrong things, then we
lie.

Burns drew a picture of William Fisher, an elder of the
Church in Mauchline; Holy Willie he called him. Burns
made him say:

> I bless and praise Thy matchless might,
> While thousands Thou hast left in night,

* Barclay adds "purity."

That I am here afore Thy sight,
    For gifts an' grace,
A burning an' a shinin' light,
    To a' this place.

This same William Fisher had stolen the Church collection, had more than once been found dead drunk in a ditch, had seduced more than one of the village girls, and yet paraded himself as one of the chosen of God. A life like that was a lie, and Burns branded him for ever as a hypocrite. We do not need to be as bad as William Fisher, but the person who says he believes in Jesus and yet lives dishonestly and impurely is not a Christian. When judged by the fruits of his life, he fails the test completely.

The first test then is the good life. This does not mean that we have to be absolutely good, no one can be that. But it does mean that we have to try, and that when we make a mistake and go wrong we have to be genuinely sorry, and have to prove that we are sorry by doing better.

ii. The second test is *love for others*. The New Testament says this again and again. Jesus said, 'By this all men will know that you are my disciples, if you have love one for another' (John 13:35). John said sternly, 'If anyone says, "I love God", and hates his brother, he is a liar' (I John 4:20).

Here is a simple test. You cannot be a Christian and hate anyone. Hatred is bad for a man. It does not only injure the man it hates, it injures even worse the man who hates. Sir Winston Churchill lived to a great age. Once in his old age he said, 'I have only managed to live so long because I have never allowed myself to have any bitterness to anyone.'

The world is full of people who are divided; even the Church is full of people who will not speak to each other. God forgave us and we must forgive others. God does not

"Love for others" is not separate from "the good life."

stop loving us even when we hurt him, and we must be like God. No man can be a Christian and hate. The mark of the Christian is that he is the friend of all.

A tree is tested by its fruits, and man must be judged by his life; and the two marks of the Christian life are personal purity and love for all.

For Discussion

How is bitterness caused? If we become bitter can anything be done about it?

The fruit tells us
something of the root,

See Luke parallel, Luke 6:43f

"Faking Sincerity" joke.

CHAPTER THIRTY

The Only Foundation

Matthew 7:24-27

With this section we reach the end of the Sermon on the Mount, and in it Jesus issues a challenge. In effect he says, 'You have heard what I have to say. What about it? Are you going to make it the basis of your whole life? Or, are you going to disregard it, or even go away and forget about it?' In our last section we saw that faith means action. For that reason no one can be neutral to Jesus. We have to accept or refuse to accept what he says, because we have got to act upon it or refuse to act upon it. We are being confronted with a call to action, and not to act on it is to refuse it.

Jesus drew a picture of two men to show how important foundations are. They each set out to build a house. One dug right down until he struck the solid rock, and on it he laid the foundations of his house. In due time the winter came with its wind and storms and floods; but this man's house was founded on the rock and was able to stand immovable, defying the worst that the weather could do.

The other man's action was not so improbable as it looks at first sight. In Palestine there were many streams which in the summer time dried up altogether. Where the stream had been there remained a pleasant little valley; it might look the very place to build a house, a sheltered hollow. So the second man found one of these apparently pleasant little hollows; he never bothered to dig down; he built on the top of the sand. This was all right as long as the summer weather lasted; but when the winter came, the pleasant hollow became

a raging torrent of foaming water, and since the house had
no foundations anyway, it collapsed in ruins.

A life is like a house; it has to be erected on some foundation; and the foundation it is erected on will make all the
difference. So Jesus is in effect asking: What is the foundation on which you have erected your life? We could completely change the metaphor, and put it in another way:
What is the driving force of your life? There could be many
answers to that.

Some people live life on the basis of doing exactly what
they like. That simply means that they are still children
and have never grown up. Sometimes if we ask a child to do
something, he will answer, 'I don't want to.' He is not old
enough to see that there are very good reasons for having to
do a great many things we don't want to do; and the person
who does only what he wants has simply never grown up.

Some people live life on the basis of ambition. They want
to succeed; they don't care how they succeed, and they don't
care how many people they hurt and how many people they
push out of the way. That is the way in which a pagan lives.
The pagan believes in the survival of the strongest and the
weakest goes to the wall. This is founded on selfishness, and
is therefore the very opposite of Christianity.

Some people live on the basis of what other people will
say about them. As it has been put, for them the voice of
their neighbours is louder than the voice of God. All that
matters to them is their reputation and their popularity. That
is not Christian because that is putting the verdict of men
above the verdict of God.

For the Christian, the driving force of life is Jesus and
obedience to his commands. We should be ready to give our
total obedience to Jesus for three reasons.

i. We should be ready to make his commands the foundation of our lives *because of what he is*. John calls him the Word (John 1:1-14). A word is the means whereby two people communicate with each other; and if Jesus is God's Word, it is through Jesus that God communicates with us. In Jesus God speaks to us; to hear Jesus speaking is to hear God speaking. We ought to obey Jesus and to make him the basis of our life because he is able to tell us the will of God.

ii. We should be ready to make his commands the foundation of life *because of what we are*. The creation story tells us that God created man in his own image (Genesis 1:27). This is to say that there is a close connection between us and God. That connection is so close that Augustine said of us all when he was praying to God, 'Our hearts are restless until they rest in thee.' This is to say that there is no real happiness for any of us except when we obey God. It is from Jesus that we learn what God's will is, and therefore, just because we are what we are, there is no happiness in anything except in obeying him.

iii. We should be ready to make his commands the foundation of life *because of what life is*. The most important fact about life is that life does not end with this world. And since Jesus knows what the life of heaven is like only he can prepare us for it. It is he who can make us able to live this life well, and who can make us fit for the life that comes after this one.

Because of what Jesus is, because of what we are, and because of what life is, it should be easy to be willing to take Jesus as the foundation of our lives.

⌐ NOT. see Mt 5:1f

For Discussion

What will it mean to us to make Jesus the foundation of life?